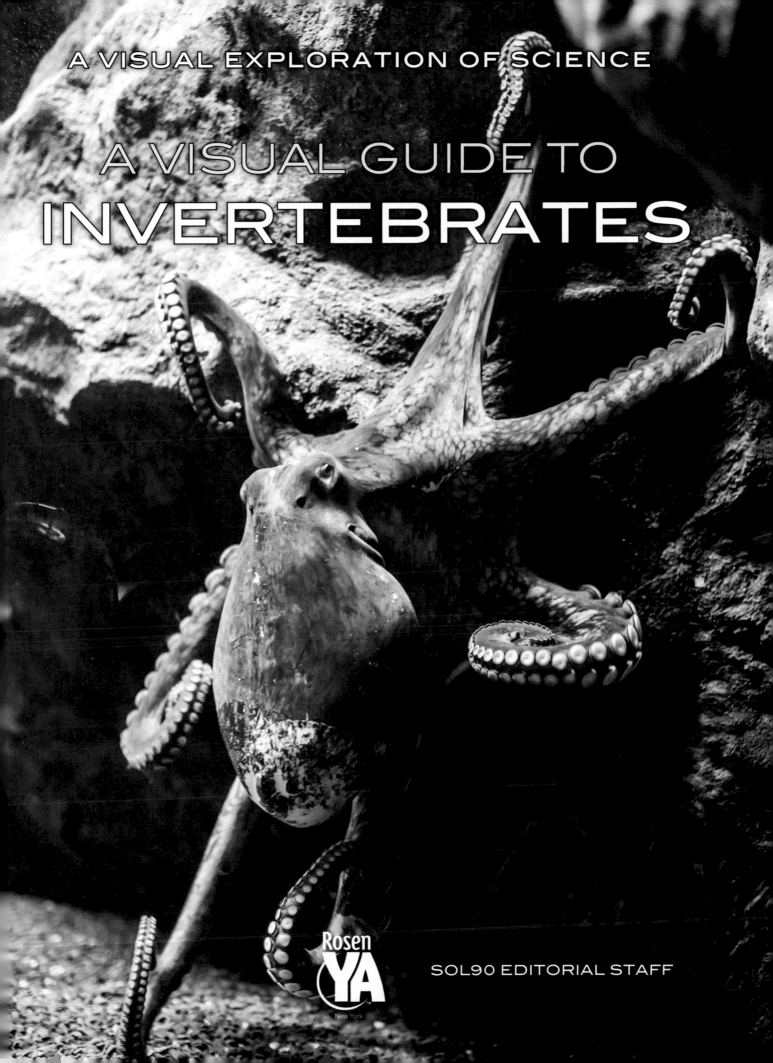

A VISUAL EXPLORATION OF SCIENCE

A VISUAL GUIDE TO
INVERTEBRATES

Rosen
YA
New York

SOL90 EDITORIAL STAFF

This edition published in 2019 by:
The Rosen Publishing Group, Inc.
29 East 21st Street
New York, NY 10010

Cataloging-in-Publication Data

Names: Editorial Sol 90 (Firm).
Title: A visual guide to invertebrates / edited by the Sol 90 Editorial Staff.
Description: New York : Rosen YA, 2019. | Series: A visual exploration of science | Includes glossary and index.
Identifiers: LCCN ISBN 9781508182375 (pbk.) | ISBN 9781508182368 (library bound)
Subjects: LCSH: Invertebrates–Juvenile literature.
Classification: LCC QL362.4 V578 2019 | DDC 592–dc23

Manufactured in the United States of America

© 2019 Editorial Sol90, S.L. Barcelona
All Rights Reserved.
Original Edition © 2009 Editorial Sol90, S.L. Barcelona

Project Management: Nuria Cicero
Editorial Coordination: Alberto Hernández, Joan Soriano, Diana Malizia
Proofreaders: Marta Kordon, Edgardo D'Elio
Layout: Laura Ocampo

Photo Credits: Age Fotostock, Getty Images, Science Photo Library, Graphic News, ESA, NASA, National Geographic, Latinstock, Album, ACI, Cordon Press, Shutterstock

Illustrators: Guido Arroyo, Pablo Aschei, Gustavo J. Caironi, Hernán Cañellas, Leonardo César, José Luis Corsetti, Vanina Farías, Manrique Fernández Buente, Joana Garrido, Celina Hilbert, Jorge Ivanovich, Isidro López, Diego Martín, Jorge Martínez, Marco Menco, Marcelo Morán, Ala de Mosca, Diego Mourelos, Eduardo Pérez, Javier Pérez, Ariel Piroyansky, Fernando Ramallo, Ariel Roldán, Marcel Socías, Néstor Taylor, Trebol Animation, Juan Venegas, Constanza Vicco, Coralia Vignau, Gustavo Yamin, 3DN, 3DOM studio.

Contents

Tiny Creatures

nvertebrates were the first forms of animal life on Earth. They are the most ancient and most numerous of known life-forms. Some, such as worms, sea anemones, and jellyfish, are soft-bodied. Others, such as insects and crustaceans, are hard-bodied. Some, including jellyfish, live in the water and swim freely. However, others, such as corals and anemones, are fixed in one place. This fascinating world of tiny creatures has over 1.5 million known species, with a wide variety of shapes and habits.

Bees are among the most important insects. They process the nectar of flowers to produce honey, a sugary liquid that humans use as a sweetener and nutrient. The nutritive component of honey is pure carbohydrate in the form of simple sugars, which are directly absorbed by the body. This characteristic gives honey its punch as a quick energy source. Edible in its natural state, it can also be used as an ingredient of desserts or to sweeten drinks. Not only bees, however, but also wasps play a fundamental role in the lives of all living beings. Many plants depend on them for pollination of their flowers. Without these insects there would be fewer fruits and vegetables to eat.

Here we show you the inside workings of a beehive. Did you know that one difference between bees and other insects is the organized communities that bees form? Keeping in mind that each artificial honeycomb has about 30,000 inhabitants, there must be a way to keep order, and the bees know by instinct how to do this. The queen, the drones, and the workers know their roles and duties well. They may even die defending the colony, just like ants, who are also true masters of order and productivity. Noteworthy in the world of insects is their high degree of evolutionary development. They are the highest achievers of the animal world. They live all over the planet, need little food to survive, and escape from predators with highly developed means of locomotion. All insects have jointed legs and an external skeleton for protection. In this book you will also be able to admire the beauty of butterflies and the changes they experience throughout their lives, and you will discover the world through the eyes of a fly. Have you heard that, among the 35,000 known species of spiders, only 30 are truly poisonous, and that without these poisonous creatures we would be swimming in a sea of insects? Also interesting are the many kinds of spiderwebs that spiders use for making traps, mating, moving about, and covering their burrows.

We invite you to explore the pages of this fact-filled book, with fascinating photos and intriguing facts about the inner and external lives of the invertebrates that share our world. Mosquitoes, for example, can pierce the skin of mammals and feed on their blood, and flies can eat solid food because their digestive process begins outside their bodies. No athlete can jump like the flea, a tiny, wingless insect that lives on the blood of birds and mammals. We will also tell you about beneficial insects that can be useful to have in your house, and about others that it would be better to control and keep away, because they can transmit sicknesses such as Chagas disease. Just turn the page to find detailed accounts along with carefully selected images that will show you in full detail how some of the smallest creatures on Earth live, change, grow, and communicate. It is well worth it!

Origin and Habitats

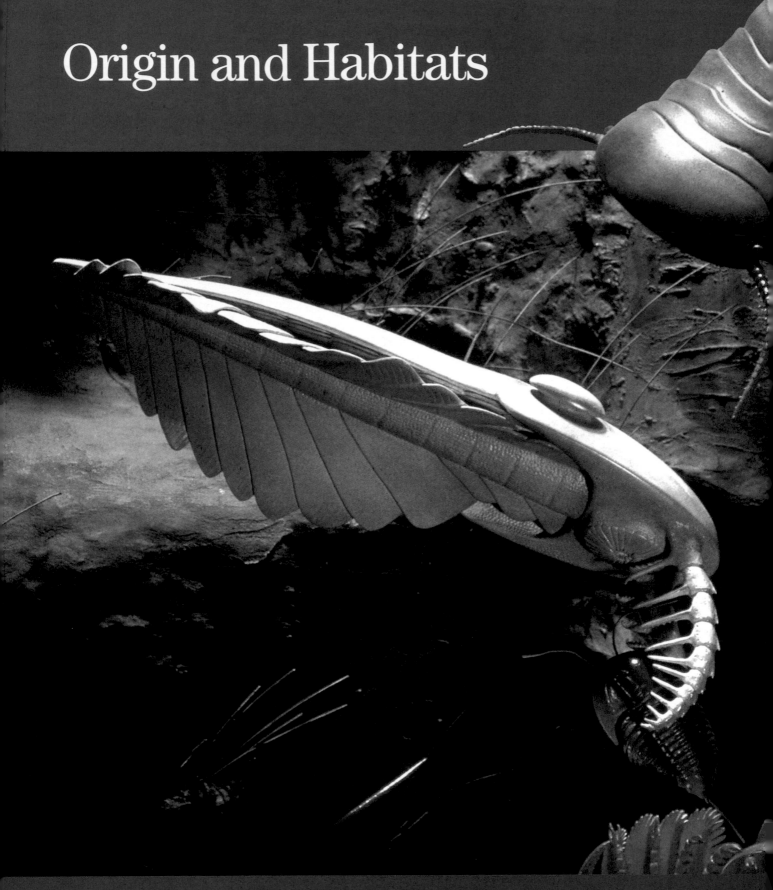

The first life-forms appeared nearly 4 billion years ago. The main groups of organisms with complex cells (eukaryotes) evolved during the Precambrian Period. Fossils found in Australia and Canada show that those invertebrates had soft bodies, quite different from those that exist today. Members of the kingdom Animalia became adapted to

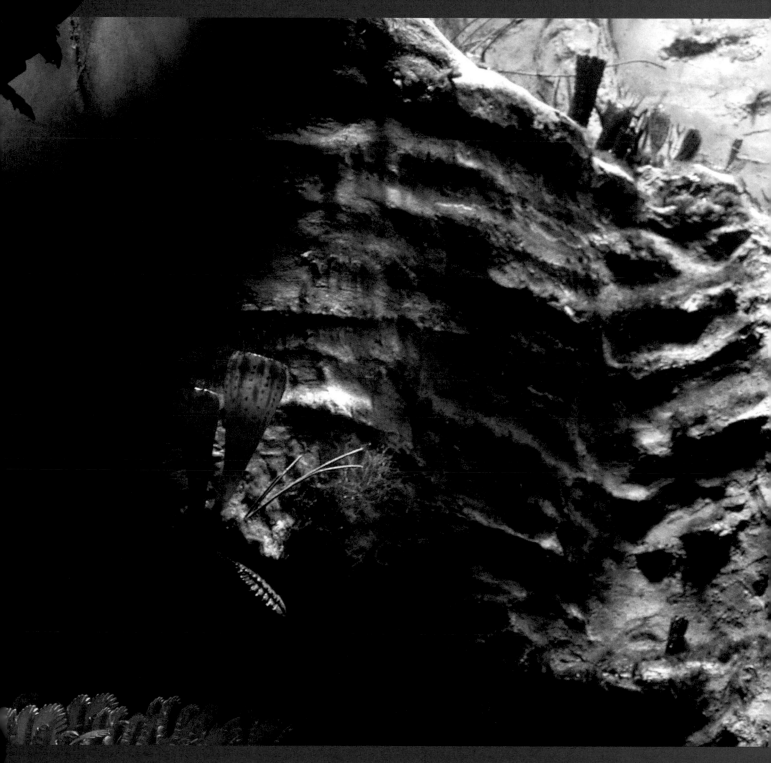

many environments, extending from the bottom of the ocean to the highest mountain peaks. We will show you the oldest species and many of the main groups of today: sponges (phylum Porifera); corals, anemones, and jellyfish (phylum Cnidaria); shellfish (phylum Mollusca); sea worms and earthworms (phylum Annelida); insects, spiders, millipedes, and crustaceans (phylum Arthropoda); and starfish and sea urchins (phylum Echinodermata). ●

Traces of Ancient Life

Millions of years ago, our planet was not as we know it today. The continents were arranged differently, and the climate, flora, and fauna were different. How do we know this? We have learned these things by finding and studying fossils, remains of past life-forms that are preserved in both geography and time. The Ediacara, in southern Australia, and the Burgess Shale, in Canada, are two regions with extensive fossil beds of soft-bodied invertebrates. Both areas have shed light on what is known as the Cambrian explosion. ●

Burgess Shale

Located in Canada, Burgess Shale is well known for its fossil bed of soft-bodied animals from the Cambrian Period. This bed gives a glimpse of what ocean life was like during the Cambrian Period, with specimens of the four main types of arthropods: trilobites, crustaceans, horseshoe crabs, and Uniramia (the group that includes insects).

540 million years
AGE OF THE FOSSILS FOUND IN THIS BED

Ediacara

This group, called Ediacara fauna, is the oldest known group of multicelled organisms. Found in Precambrian rock, it predates the great Cambrian explosion. Its age is around 600 million years; it contains impressions, or molds, of diverse animal forms conserved in sedimentary rock, without a trace of hard parts. The first such bed was found in southern Australia, in the Ediacara Hills.

DICKINSONIA SPECIES
Believed to belong to the Cnidarian (coral, jellyfish, anemones) or Annelid (worms) phyla. The largest was 17 inches (43 cm) long.

CANADA
Latitude 51° 25′ 30″ N
Longitude 116° 30′ 00″ W

This fossil bed is outstanding for the variety of creatures found.

600 million years
AGE OF THE FIRST SPECIMENS FOUND

AUSTRALIA
Latitude 35° 15′ S
Longitude 149° 28′ E

The first specimens were found in the Ediacara Hills.

JELLYFISH
Ediacaran

CHARNIA
One of the most widely found fossils of the Ediacaran Period. It is believed to have been related to certain cnidarian colonies.

EVOLUTION

Trilobites are the best–known fossilized animals to appear during the Cambrian explosion. The fossil record shows an extraordinary proliferation of life–forms during this stage of life on Earth. From this time on, no new structures of morphological organization appeared. Rather, existing forms evolved and diversified.

Olenoides

Xandarella

Emeraldella

Yohoia

Sidneyia

Burgessia

AYSHEAIA
From 0.5 to 2.5 inches (1–6 cm) long.

OPABINIA
From 1.5 to 3 inches (4–7 cm) long.

CHANCELLORIA
This cylindrical form is thought to have possibly been a sponge.

ANOMALOCARIS
20 inches (50 cm) long.

CANADIA
Estimated to have been between 0.8 and 2.0 inches (2–5 cm) long.

WIWAXIA
A rare marvel with no known biological relationship to any other life-form.

OTTOIA
This priapulid worm could measure up to 3 inches (8 cm) long.

MARRELLA SPLENDENS
Less than 1 inch long, this creature is thought to live on the seafloor.

SIZES

The Burgess Shale invertebrates had a wide range of sizes, from microscopic to nearly 7 feet (2 m) long. (Dogs, on the other hand, have a narrower size range; the most common breeds range from 20 to 40 inches [50 -100 cm] tall.)

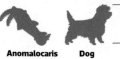

Anomalocaris   **Dog**

20 inches (50 cm)

FOSSILS

Fossils yield clues about life in the past. By comparing fossilized organisms from different periods of the Earth's history with organisms of today, we can deduce how various life-forms have changed over time.

Trilobite

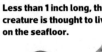

Frozen in Time

Fossils give evidence about many different ancient life-forms. Bones, footprints, and other signs of animal and plant life can become fossils as their organic components are replaced by mineral compounds. Many arthropods were trapped in the sap of certain trees. When this sticky substance hardened, it became what is called amber. Amber is very useful for studying processes that gave rise to the diversity of life on Earth. ●

Value

Amber containing animals that lived millions of years ago is used to make jewelry. Its price depends on the type of organism it contains.

FOSSIL IN AMBER
Photograph of amber that contains fossil remains from 38 million years ago. This piece is valued at nearly $35,000.

FOSSILIZED ARACHNID
This spider, perfectly conserved thanks to the protection of the amber, enables scientists to make reliable comparisons with genera and species of today.

Diverse Origins

➤ The color of fossilized amber depends on the type of tree it came from, when it was formed, and the environment where it was fossilized. Amber is usually yellow, although it may come in many shades ranging from orange, red, brown, blue, and green to transparent varieties. Although color is important, amber is classified according to its origin.

Mineral deposit	Origin	Shades
Baltic	Eocene conifers	
Burma	Eocene Burseraceans	
Dominican Republic	Miocene legumes	
Sicily	Miocene Burseraceans	
Romania	Miocene legumes	
Mexico	Miocene legumes	
Canada	Cretaceous conifers	

572° F
(300° C)

The melting point of amber

Properties and Characteristics

➤ Amber is a material derived from the fossilized resin of certain trees that lived between 65 and 144 million years ago. Over time they were fossilized, forming large, irregular masses within layers of sandstone and slate mixed with clay. Masses of amber range from very small, only a fraction of an inch, to many times longer, up to 20 inches (50 cm) in length, with a hardness of 2 to 3 on the Mohs scale. Amber is composed of carbon, oxygen, and hydrogen.

1

During the Cretaceous and Tertiary Periods, forests covered a wide area. The trees secreted a resinous substance that oozed out in the form of drops.

2

This substance accumulated on tree branches and bark and at the foot of the trunk, trapping all sorts of plants and animals (even toads) that got stuck in the thick resin.

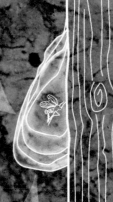

3

The resin insulated the animal from the atmosphere and protected its remains from water and air. As the resin hardened, it gradually formed a protective, pressure-resistant layer. Over time this layer was transformed into what we know today as amber.

Ancient Life-Forms

➤ Finding these fossilized creatures enables us to learn about life-forms and environments of the past. The presence of certain fossils can help us to determine what the climate was like millions of years ago and to date rock layers. We know that certain plants and animals lived in specific periods. Their presence or absence can help us determine the age of the rock layer where they are found. Not only did amber preserve plants and animals, but it also trapped air bubbles.

The First Conquest

To be able to live on land, invertebrates developed ways of breathing and moving that were adapted to a land environment. Thus insects, which can walk and fly, have populated land and air environments. Other invertebrates have also become accustomed to life in this element, and they play an important role in land ecosystems.●

MONARCH BUTTERFLY
Danaus plexippus

ASIAN TIGER MOSQUITO
Aedes albopictus

CRAMER'S BLUE MORPHO
Morpho rhetenor

PRAYING MANTIS
Family Mantidae

70% OF THE SPECIES THAT LIVE IN TREES ARE INSECTS.

Who Eats Whom?

The relationships of eating and being eaten that are established among the organisms of an ecosystem are called the food chain. In contrast to plants, whose capacity for photosynthesis gives them the role of food producers, invertebrates occupy various levels in the food chain as food consumers.

THE ORDER OF THE FOOD CHAIN

Aphids

Ladybugs

Spiders

1 FIRST LEVEL
Invertebrates that eat plants

2 SECOND LEVEL
Carnivores that eat herbivorous invertebrates

3 THIRD LEVEL
Larger invertebrates that eat other carnivorous invertebrates

The Most Successful

Beetles (order Coleoptera) are the most prolific and diverse group of the animal kingdom. This is mostly because of their chitinous exoskeletons and highly compact elytras (wing covers), which give each species the hardness, flexibility, texture, or color it needs to adapt to its environment.

OVER
350,000
SPECIES OF B
ARE KNOW

COMMON FURNITURE   Tunnels bored
BEETLE *Anobium*   by beetles
punctatum

FEEDING ON
DEAD MATTER

TICK
Boophilus sp.

SILVERFISH
Lepisma saccharina

Small Arthropods

Most land- and air-dwelling arthropods have a tracheal respiratory system consisting of highly efficient air tubes that supply oxygen directly to the cells and tissues. The tracheal system makes it possible for these arthropods to maintain a high metabolic rate, but it also tends to limit body size. That is why land-dwelling arthropods are relatively small compared to the rest of the animal kingdom.

PAPER WASP
Polistes

EUROPEAN HORNET
Vespa crabro

BROWN
GARDEN SNAIL
Helix aspersa

BURYING
BEETLE
*Nicrophorus
investigator*

BLACK VINE
WEEVIL
*Otiorhynchus
sulcatus*

CLICK
BEETLE
Agriotes lineatus

CENTIPEDE
Lithobius

PILLBUGS
Armadillium

DESERT MILLIPEDE
Orthoporus ornatus

BLOOD-RED
ANT (WORKER)
Formica sanguinea

Naturally
Programmed

The world of air- and land-dwelling invertebrates includes societies, such as those of bees, wasps, and ants (order Hymenoptera). The bees' dances to inform other bees about the location of new food sources, their strict division of labor, or the structure of a spiderweb correspond to patterns of behavior specific to each species. Each individual carries these patterns inscribed within, like a computer program that executes perfectly.

SPIDER
Drassodes

SILKWORM
Bombyx mori

EARTHWORM
Lumbricus

Life Began in the Sea

| nvertebrates are not defined by any single common characteristic, but simply by not being vertebrates. Their heterogeneity is most notable in the ocean. Some 3.8 billion years ago, life arose in our planet's oceans. The species that inhabit the ocean waters show greater diversity than those found in other environments. Some forms of animal life, such as corals and sponges, are so simple that they are not able to move about on their own. Others, such as some cephalopods, show great intelligence and skill. ●

A World Without Insects

Arthropods are the most prolific animals on the planet. But just as insects (hexapods) reign on land, crustaceans have been successful in the water. They breathe through gills, and some, such as krill, are microscopic. Most, however, are larger than insects–mostly because they have no need of complex and costly metamorphosis.

CARAMOTE
PRAWN
***Penaeus
kerathurus***

AMERICAN
LOBSTER
Homarus americanus

CORAL

Acropora
Coral reefs are
environments inhabited
by thousands of ocean
creatures. They make up
their own ecosystem.

The Largest

The reduced effects of gravity in the water enable the largest invertebrates to live in the sea. Out of the water, octopus and squid–cephalopod mollusks with no rigid structure or joints in their bodies–would not be able to move or hold themselves up, let alone hunt. Perhaps this is why no invertebrates of this size are found on land.

50,000
THE VAST MAJORITY LIVE
IN THE SEA

BROADCLUB
CUTTLEFISH
Sepia latimanus

ANTARCTIC
KRILL
***Euphausia
superba***

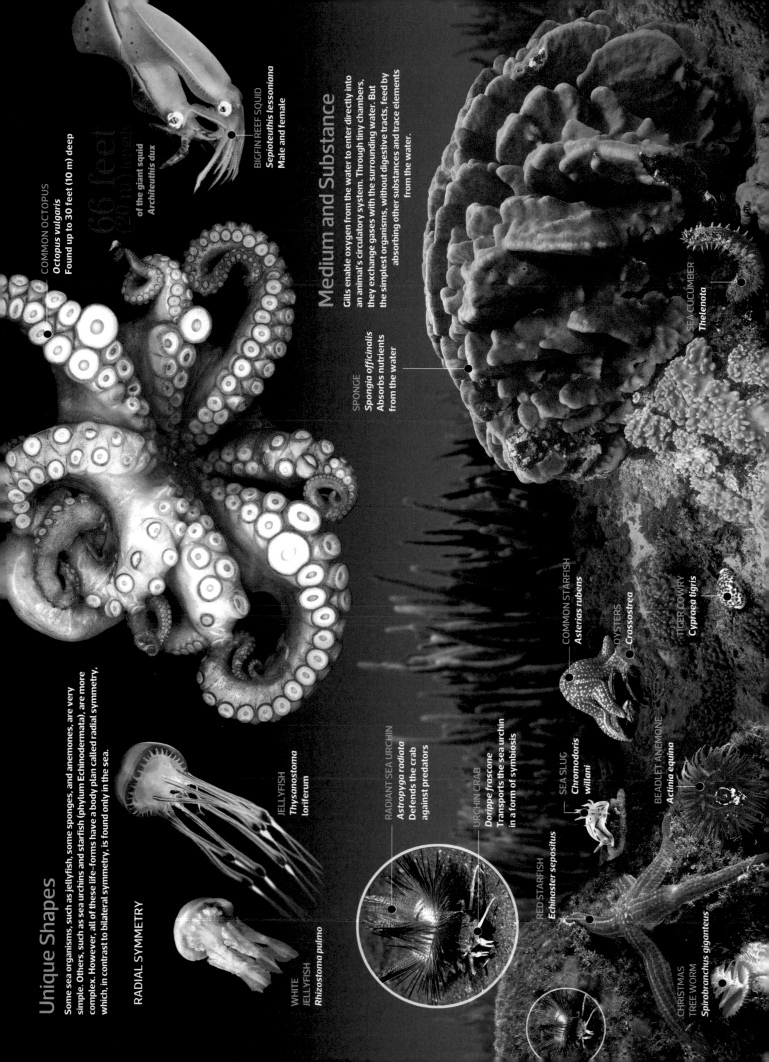

Unique Shapes

Some sea organisms, such as jellyfish, some sponges, and anemones, are very simple. Others, such as sea urchins and starfish (phylum Echinodermata), are more complex. However, all of these life-forms have a body plan called radial symmetry, which, in contrast to bilateral symmetry, is found only in the sea.

RADIAL SYMMETRY

COMMON OCTOPUS
Octopus vulgaris
Found up to 30 feet (10 m) deep

BIGFIN REEF SQUID
Sepioteuthis lessoniana
Male and female

66 feet
(20 m) length
of the giant squid
Architeuthis dux

JELLYFISH
Thysanostoma loriferum

WHITE
JELLYFISH
Rhizostoma pulmo

Medium and Substance

Gills enable oxygen from the water to enter directly into an animal's circulatory system. Through tiny chambers, they exchange gases with the surrounding water. But the simplest organisms, without digestive tracts, feed by absorbing other substances and trace elements from the water.

SPONGE
Spongia officinalis
Absorbs nutrients
from the water

SEA CUCUMBER
Thelenota

RADIANT SEA URCHIN
Astropyga radiata
Defends the crab
against predators

URCHIN CRAB
Dorippe frascone
Transports the sea urchin
in a form of symbiosis

COMMON STARFISH
Asterias rubens

OYSTERS
Crassostrea

SEA SLUG
Chromodoris willani

BEADLET ANEMONE
Actinia equina

TIGER COWRY
Cypraea tigris

RED STARFISH
Echinaster sepositus

CHRISTMAS
TREE WORM
Spirobranchus giganteus

Teeming Freshwater Environments

In rivers, ponds, lakes, lagoons, and swamps, many invertebrate species are adapted to life in the water but come from other habitats. Thus, water beetles breathe, not with gills, but with spiracles, the way land insects do. This means they must obtain a reserve of air or come to the surface to breathe. Crustaceans have mechanisms that protect them from losing salt in fresh water. With these adaptations, invertebrates make seemingly calm waters the scene of an intense struggle to survive. ●

One Species, Two Environments

Many species of land- and air-dwelling insects lay their eggs in water. After hatching, the larvae undergo metamorphosis in the water. This fact has enabled certain species to prosper by colonizing more than one environment at once. Not only does the same individual inhabit different environments at different stages of its life, but it also has distinct feeding habits and means of breathing during those stages. That fact keeps adults of the species from competing with the young for food.

MAYFLY
Hexagenia

WATER MEASURER
Hydrometra stagnorum

8% OF INSECTS LIVE IN WATER.

LIFE CYCLE OF THE COMMON MOSQUITO

1 EGGS
After feeding on blood, adult females lay 40 to 400 eggs on the surface of the water.

2 LARVAE
After one week, the eggs hatch and the larvae are born.

3 PUPAE
The larva molts four times as it grows, finally reaching the pupa stage.

4 ADULT
After a few days the pupa's skin splits and the adult mosquito emerges. The adult will live for only a few weeks.

THE PROCESS LASTS ABOUT ONE MONTH

On the Border

The areas in and around water and close to the water's surface are the scenes of a battle for survival. Most freshwater insects live in this zone.

DRAGONFLY NYMPH
Molting dragonfly

EMPEROR DRAGONFLY
Anax imperator
The adults feed on small flying insects that live near plants by the shore of bodies of fresh water.

COMMON POND SKATER
Gerris lacustris
Lives in water. It has just the right weight and structure to take advantage of surface tension when the water is calm.

WATER BOATMAN (BACK SWIMMER)
Notonecta glauca

Adapted to the Water

Some water species breathe through air tubes or tracheae. All such organisms had to develop a mechanism or device for providing themselves with air, because tracheae and tracheoles are useless for breathing underwater.

GREAT POND SNAIL
Lymnaea stagnalis

GREAT DIVING BEETLE
Dytiscus marginalis

CADDISFLY LARVA
Limnephilus

COPEPOD
Cyclops

MEDICINAL LEECH
Hirudo medicinalis

ZOOPLANKTON

DIVING BELL SPIDER
Argyroneta aquatica

Living Off Others

Some organisms are parasites. They do not obtain their own food; rather, they live at the expense of another species. Although they depend on another animal for sustenance, they avoid doing the other species too much harm. Otherwise, the parasite would have to find a new host.

TRICHODINA
Trichodina fultoni

BLOOD-FLUKES (BILHARZIA)
Schistosoma

Most parasitic worms are microscopic in size. The ones shown here are highly magnified.

WHITE-CLAWED CRAYFISH
Austropotamobius pallipes
Glands on its antennae excrete water and maintain the balance of salts in its body.

WATER BEETLE LARVA

DRAGONFLY NYMPH

In Fresh Water

Ocean invertebrates live in an osmotic balance between water and the salts the water contains. Invertebrates that live in estuaries or other places where salt water receives currents of fresh water (euryhaline organisms) must keep the concentration of salts in their bodies constant, even when the salinity of the water changes. In fresh water, with its low concentration of salt, crustaceans developed mechanisms to eliminate water and capture salts actively–that is, their bodies expend energy on these functions. For this reason river crustaceans, unlike sea crustaceans, urinate.

The Simplest Life-Forms

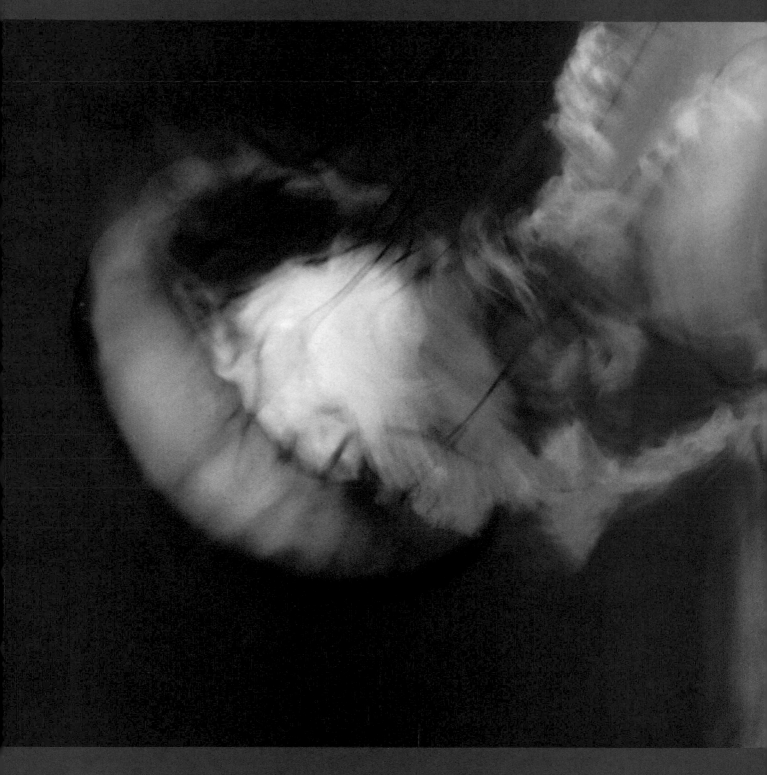

Even though most organisms such as sponges, jellyfish, and sea anemones look like vegetables, they belong to the animal kingdom. Many of these simple invertebrates are unable to move from one place to another; some even lack certain tissues or an entire respiratory or digestive system. Other, more developed species, such as

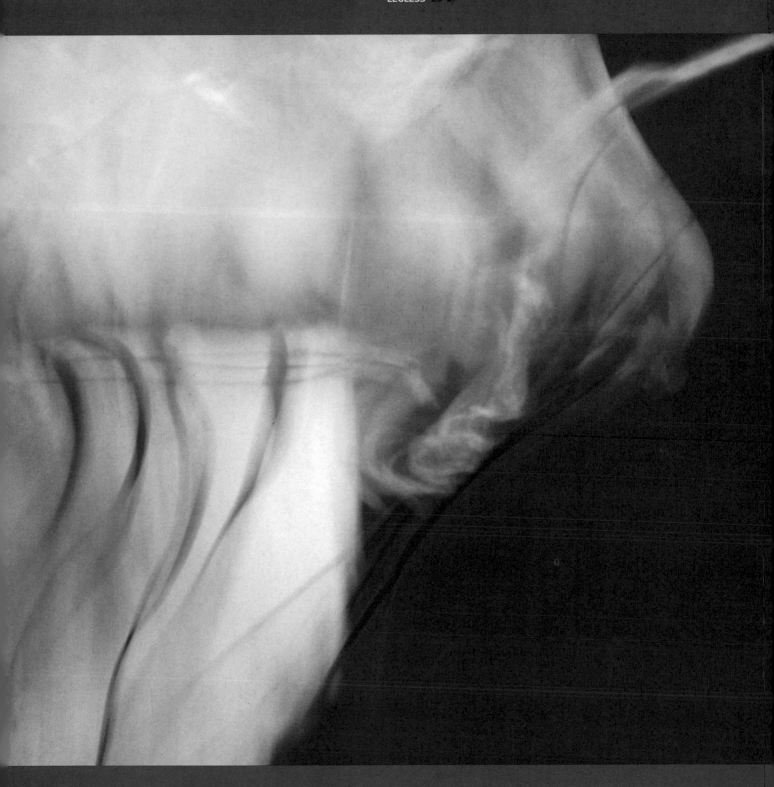

squid and octopus, can move about and have become skilled marine predators. Cephalopods are the most highly evolved mollusks. Their heads have highly developed eyes, a mouth with two horn-like jaws, and tentacles with suckers to trap their prey. Some cephalopods live in deep-sea waters, whereas others stay close to shore. ●

Radial Symmetry

Many of the numerous invertebrates on Earth live in the ocean. Some, such as polyps and jellyfish, have radial symmetry–that is, their bodies are structured around an axis. A typical echinoderm such as the starfish has tiny, flexible, tube-shaped legs arranged like the spokes of a wheel. The animal uses them to hold onto surfaces and to move. Sponges, on the other hand, are very simple, multiple-celled animals, with many small pores that they use to feed.●

RADIAL SYMMETRY

The body parts are organized around a central axis like the spokes on the wheel of a bicycle. Any plane passing through the body will divide it into two halves, each mirroring the other.

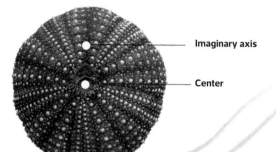

Imaginary axis

Center

SEA URCHIN
Strongylocentrotus franciscanus

Echinoderms

This phylum includes sea lilies, sea cucumbers, urchins, and starfish. The echinoderms have an internal skeleton made of calcified plates and a locomotion system made up of ambulacral grooves with rows of tube feet. In most echinoderm species, the endoskeleton is made of tiny calcareous plates held together by skin and muscle tissue.

ECHINODERM means that this animal's body is covered by a spiny skin.

ECHINODERM CLASSES

ECHINOIDEA
Sea urchins

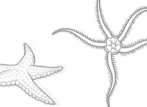

ASTEROIDEA
Starfish

OPHIUROIDEA
Brittle stars

CRINOIDEA
Sea lilies

HOLOTHUROIDEA
Sea cucumbers

THERE ARE APPROXIMATELY

7,000

LIVING SPECIES AND 13,000 EXTINCT SPECIES OF ECHINODERMS.

Cnidarians

Cnidarians are a group of aquatic animals that includes jellyfish, hydras, sea anemones, and corals. Their cells are organized in true tissues. They have specialized cells called cnidoblasts for stinging prey and for defense. Two basic types of cnidarians are polyps and jellyfish.

JELLYFISH
Pelagia noctiluca

CLASSIFICATION

HYDROZOA:
Asexual polyp

ANTHOZOA: Sea anemones and corals

SCYPHOZOA: Jellyfish

Mesoglea
Gastrovascular cavity
Mouth
Gastrodermis
Epidermis

STINGING CELL
Used for defense

1 INTACT
Cnidocyst
Nucleus
Operculum
Cnidocilium

2 DISCHARGING
Rolled-up tube
Barb

3 DISCHARGED
Unfolded stinging tube

REPRODUCTION

6 JELLYFISH
The polyp's body grows and begins to form jellyfish, which pile up like a stack of plates.

Young jellyfish

Adult jellyfish

Most common habitat
COASTS OF THE UNITED STATES

1 GAMETES
Adult jellyfish produce sperm and egg cells during meiosis and then release them.

2 FERTILIZATION
Fertilization takes place in the waters near the jellyfish, resulting in a zygote.

5 POLYP
The planula larva settles at the bottom, where it attaches to a surface. There it develops a mouth and tentacles, and transforms into a polyp.

3 BLASTULA
The zygote, after a series of cell divisions, becomes a blastula, or hollow sphere, of cells.

THERE ARE APPROXIMATELY

9,000
SPECIES OF CNIDARIANS (COELENTERATES).

4 PLANULA
The blastula lengthens and becomes a ciliated larva called a planula.

Porifera

...e sessile aquatic animals. Most live at the bottom ...the ocean, although there are some freshwater ...ecies. They are the simplest animals, lacking organs ...true tissues, and their cells are independent to ...ertain extent. They are basically water-filtering ...dies formed by one or more cavities. Most porifera ...ve no definite shape, but some have radial ...mmetry.

THERE ARE APPROXIMATELY

5,000
SPECIES (150 ARE FRESHWATER, AND THE REST ARE MARINE).

Water coming out

Oscula

Epithelial cell

Spicule

The water with food particles enters through the porocytes.

...PES OF PORIFERA ACCORDING ...ORGANIZATION

→ Direction of water flow

Nucleus

Flagellum

ASCON

SYCON

LEUCON

Sea Carnival

Corals and anemones, together with jellyfish, make up the phylum Cnidaria. Some characteristics they share are their bright colors, tentacles that secrete stinging substances, and a digestive system with a common opening for ingestion and excretion–the simplest digestive system in the animal kingdom. All of these organisms are quite simple. Corals generally form colonies, large groups of small polyps that stay practically immobile and feed on microorganisms brought to them by water currents. Sea anemones, on the other hand, are solitary and can trap prey despite their limited locomotion. ●

CORAL
POLYP

Coral Reefs

Corals are small polyps with tentacles that grow at their base throughout their life, generating a calcareous exoskeleton. This skeleton forms masses, or branches. Most corals grow in colonies; the skeletons form huge calcareous masses called reefs. Corals live mostly in warm, shallow ocean waters. Their reproduction can be both sexual and asexual, by division or by gemmation. They feed on plankton.

HARD CORALS
grow over the surface of the lime–bearing substrate.

SOFT CORALS
branch out; their skeleton is not lime-based but horn-like and flexible.

CORAL WALLS
Even though some coral walls live alone, most form colonies that can grow upward at up to 3 feet (1 m) every year.

100 feet
(30 m)
THE MOST COMMON DEPTH AT WHICH CORALS GROW

Tentacles
with stinging cells

Mouth
Through here the animal ingests its food and excretes wastes.

Hard skeleton
A mass that grows by the accumulation of dead polyps

Live tissue

Connecting tissue
Connects one polyp with another

Gastric cavity
Divided into several cavities in hydropolyps

Calcium carbonate

Beautiful but Deadly

Beautiful for their shapes and colors that vary even within the same species, and dangerous for the poison they use to sting both victims and predators, sea anemones live in almost all marine latitudes, and at varying depths. Tropical marine anemones can measure up to 3 feet (1 m). They have a basal disc, which allows some species to attach to rocks, and others to slither, and still others to penetrate the seafloor. They trap live prey, even fish, with the many tentacles around their mouths.

9,000
THE NUMBER OF CNIDARIAN SPECIES IN THE WORLD

ADAPTATION OF SHAPE

To avoid being swept away in the current, the sea anemone retracts on sensing a water flow.

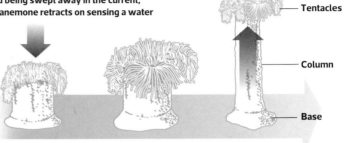

Water flow

Tentacles

Column

Base

CONTRACTION
The sea anemone reduces its size.

DISTENSION
By means of the retractor muscle

EXTENSION
When the water is calm

TENTACLES
With stinging cells, to hunt and move

CLOWNFISH
Inexplicably, the sea anemone's poison does not affect this species.

ORAL DISC

MOUTH

SEPTAL PERFORATION

INCOMPLETE MESENTERIUM

MESENTERIUM FILAMENT

RETRACTOR MUSCLE

PHARYNX

COMPLETE MESENTERIUM

GASTROVASCULAR CAVITY

SEA ANEMONE
Any vertical plane passing through its center divides it into two equal parts.

BASAL DISC

Aquatic

Echinoderms (phylum Echinodermata) are one of the best-known groups of marine invertebrates. Sea urchins and starfish, despite their apparent differences, are part of the same group and share characteristics such as five-radial symmetry. This phylum has an aquatic vascular system with many ambulacral grooves with tube feet, which it uses for locomotion, capturing prey, and breathing. In addition, it has an internal skeleton made of calcareous plates. These creatures lack a brain or eyes, so they use photoreceptors to sense movement.●

Ambulacral Grooves

These structures are hollow cylinders with thick walls that straighten and move when a starfish injects water into certain vesicles in its body. The ambulacral grooves end in suckers that the animal uses to attach itself to objects, enabling it to move at surprising speed. These sensitive feet shrink if touched abruptly, hiding behind a rim of rigid spines that protect them from harm.

570
million years
THE LENGTH OF TIME ECHINODERMS HAVE BEEN IN EXISTENCE

STOMACH

ESOPHAGUS

MOUTH
Surrounds the food and breaks it down with stomach juices

SAC
Fills with water, expands, and clings to the surface

RADIAL CANAL
The water passes and circulates to the sacs.

SKIN
The underside is covered by spines.

Suction

The sac contracts and puts pressure on the ambulacral groove. The muscles tense and force the water back into the sac, causing suction between the groove and the surface with which it makes contact.

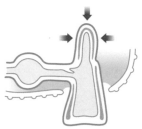

Sucker

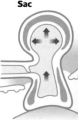

Sac

Closed valve

Substrate

Defense System

Characterized by complete five-sided symmetry, sea urchins' bodies are covered by several mobile spines that give them a dangerous appearance. The spines are spread evenly throughout the skeleton's surface and are used as a defense system.

6,000
THE NUMBER OF ECHINODERM SPECIES

SEA URCHIN
Astropyga radiata

SPINES
There are two varieties of spines: larger primary spines and shorter secondary spines. They are usually cylindrical with a narrowed tip.

BARB
Used for defense

PYLORIC CONDUIT
Moves the water that ends at the pyloric cecum, which functions as a digestive gland

STARFISH
Archaster typicus

3 The muscles can make the tube feet move to either side, and the coordinated movement of all the feet in one direction causes the starfish to advance.

2 The area near the sucker secretes an adhesive substance that helps keep it attached to the surface. The lateral muscles in the groove contract, and the liquid returns to the sac for locomotion.

Stages of Movement

The ambulacral groove and tube feet allow the starfish to perform the movements it needs for locomotion. The feet are arranged in two parallel lines along the arm, and the feet at the other end have a sensory function, monitoring the substrate over which the creature moves.

1 When the sac muscles contract, they force the liquid to pass to the ambulacral groove, which lengthens and makes contact with an adjacent surface, or substrate.

Legless

Worms are invertebrates with long, soft bodies and no legs. They are classified into three phyla. Flatworms are the simplest type; most are parasites, although some are free-living. Nematodes have a cylindrical body with a hard outer surface. Segmented worms are more complex; they include leeches, earthworms, and sea worms. Many species have an impact on plants, animals, and humans.●

Classes of Worms

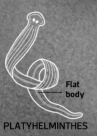

Flat body

PLATYHELMINTHES

Round body

NEMATODA

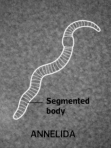

Segmented body

ANNELIDA

WORM
Nematode enoplida

Movement Guided by Light

Flatworms have eyespots, or light-sensitive eyes, on the front end of their bodies. When exposed to excessive light, the eyes withdraw and remain immobile.

EPIDERMIS

PROBOSCIS
Partly folded inward

Digestive System

In annelid worms, the digestive system extends in a straight line from the oral opening to the anus. It includes the mouth, muscular pharynx, esophagus, crop, gizzard, and intestine.

HOOKS
Hold the worm in place

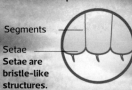

Hearts

Clitellum

Mouth Pharynx

Reproductive system

Intestine

28 feet
(8.5 m)

LENGTH OF THE LONGEST WORM: *PLACENTONEMA GIGANTISSIMUM*

EARTHWORM
Lumbricus terrestris

LOCOMOTION
Snake-like undulations along the dorsal-ventral plane

Segments

Setae
Setae are bristle-like structures.

Anus

Tissues

are formed in layers and are based on the presence of internal cavities. This annelid has three layers and one cavity, the coelom, which carries fluids through the body like a hydraulic skeleton.

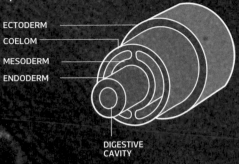

ECTODERM
COELOM
MESODERM
ENDODERM

DIGESTIVE CAVITY

FOOD
Bacteria and organic wastes

AT LEAST
100,000
KNOWN WORM SPECIES

NECK
Retracts and remains hidden

Reproduction

Flatworms and annelids are usually hermaphrodites; nematodes usually have separate sexes. In some cases the worm splits into two, resulting in two new worms.

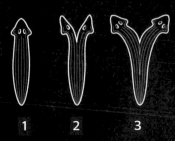

1   2   3

TISSUE
Fibrous and elastic

LEMNISCI
Food storage

SPINES
Pierce the wall of the host

Jointless

The body of most mollusks is soft, extremely flexible, and without joints, yet has a large and very hard shell. Most mollusks live in the ocean, but they are also found in lakes and land environments. All modern mollusks have bilateral symmetry, one cephalopod foot with sensory organs and locomotion, a visceral mass, and a covering, called the mantel, that secretes the shell. Mollusks also have a very peculiar mouth structure called a radula. ●

Gastropods

These mollusks are characterized by their large ventral foot, whose wave-like motions are used to move from place to place. The group comprises snails and slugs, and they can live on land, in the ocean, and in fresh water. When these animals have a shell, it is a single spiral-shaped piece, and the extreme flexibility of the rest of the body allows the gastropod to draw itself up completely within the shell. Gastropods have eyes and one or two pairs of tentacles on their head.

BROWN GARDEN SNAIL
Helix aspersa

DIGESTIVE GLAND

INTESTINE

LUNG

GONAD

KIDNEY

HEART

SALIVARY GLAND

ESOPHAGUS

PROSOBRANCHIA
This mollusk subclass mainly includes marine animals. Some have mother-of-pearl on the inside of their shell, whereas others have a substance similar to porcelain.

LUNGED
Snails, land slugs, and freshwater slugs have lungs, and their lung sacs allow them to breathe oxygen in the atmosphere.

OPISTHOBRANCHIA
are sea slugs, which are characterized by having a very small shell or no shell at all.

SEA ANGEL
Candida

BENDING OF THE SNAIL
In snails, bending is a very special phenomenon that moves the cavity of the mantle from the rear toward the front of the body. The visceral organs rotate 180 degrees, and the digestive tube and the nervous connections cross in a figure eight.

Gills

Nervous system

Digestive tract

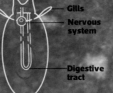

Bivalves

Mollusks with a shell divided into two halves. The two parts of the shell are joined by an elastic ligament that opens the shell, adductor muscles that close the shell, and the umbo, a system of ridges that helps the shell shut together. Almost all bivalves feed on microorganisms. Some bury themselves in the wet sand, digging small tunnels that let in water and food. The tunnels can be from a fraction of an inch long to over a yard long.

SCALLOP
Pecten jacobaeus

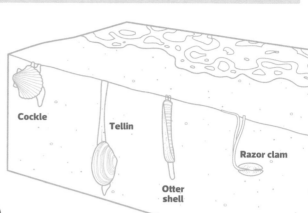

Cockle

Tellin

Razor clam

Otter shell

LAMELLIBRANCHIATA include most bivalves. They use gills to breathe and to feed. They have no differentiated head, eyes, or extremities. They can grow up to 5 inches (13 cm) long, and they rest on the ocean floor.

GREEN MUSSEL
Perna viridis

PROTOBRANCHIA
This class includes bivalves with a split lower foot, called a sole. Bivalves use their gills only to breathe. This subclass includes small bivalves 0.5 inch (13 mm) wide, called nutclams (*Nucula nitidosa*).

Under the Sand

Many mollusks live buried under the sand in order to hide from predators and the effects of waves, wind, and sudden changes in temperature.

100,000
THE NUMBER OF LIVING MOLLUSK SPECIES; AS MANY MORE HAVE BECOME EXTINCT

RADULA

FEMALE SEXUAL ORGAN

Cephalopods

Cuttlefish, octopus, squid, and nautilus are called cephalopods because their extremities, or tentacles, are attached directly to their heads. These predators are adapted to life in the oceans, and they have quite complex nervous, sensory, and motion systems. Their tentacles surround their mouths, which have a radula and a powerful beak. Cephalopods can be 0.4 inch (1 cm) long to several yards long.

NAUTILOIDEA
This subclass populated the oceans of the Paleozoic and Mesozoic periods, but today only one genus– Nautilus–survives. A nautilus has an outer shell, four gills, and ten tentacles. Its shell is made from calcium, is spiral in shape, and is divided into chambers.

NAUTILUS
Nautilus

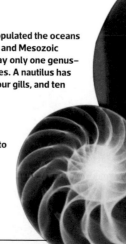

COLEOIDEA
Cephalopods of this class have a very small internal shell, or none at all, and only two gills. Except for the nautilus, this class includes all cephalopods alive today–octopus, cuttlefish, and squid.

COMMON CUTTLEFISH
Sepia officinalis

Generating Added Value

Bivalves are sought after and cultivated for their pearls. Pearls are said to be the queen of gems, because they were discovered over 4,000 years ago and were used as important symbols in many ancient cultures. In spite of their high price, pearls start out as a nuisance for the animal that creates them, which could be an oyster, a clam, or a mussel. Oysters produce the most valuable pearls, which are noted for their luster.

Pearl Formation

Occasionally grains of sand or parasites accidentally become lodged in an oyster's body and cannot escape. To relieve the annoyance, the oyster begins a defensive action and secretes a smooth, hard, crystalline substance called nacre around the object. Cultured pearls are formed from particles that are intentionally inserted into an oyster.

SHELL
Composed of two pieces or valves

INNER SURFACE
OF THE SHELL
Sensory tentacles enable the oyster to detect light and darkness.

1

INCUBATION
Pearl cultivation began in Japan. It consists of inserting into the body of a live oyster a small, round particle made from the shell of a freshwater bivalve. The oyster secretes mother-of-pearl substances from a gland in its liver to cover the object, and the pearl begins to grow.

A Introduction of foreign body

Grain of sand

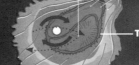

B The oyster secretes nacre to cover it.

Tongue

2

GROWTH OF THE PEARL
New, uniform layers are constantly added to the pearl, and the cultivator leaves the pearl in place until it reaches the required diameter and quality. During the process, humans intervene only to provide the oysters in farms with the right temperature, water currents, and cleanliness to favor the growth of pearls.

3 to 8 years
TIME IT TAKES FOR A PEARL TO GROW

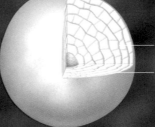

Organic layer

Aragonite crystal

LAYERS OF NACRE ON THE PEARL

LAYERS OF NACRE ON THE SHELL

Oysters

Tied with ropes

HANGING OYSTERS
These oysters are suspended from bamboo rafts in areas with abundant plankton.

Types of pearls

They can be round or elongated like a grain of rice.

NATURAL PEARL

CULTURED PEARLS

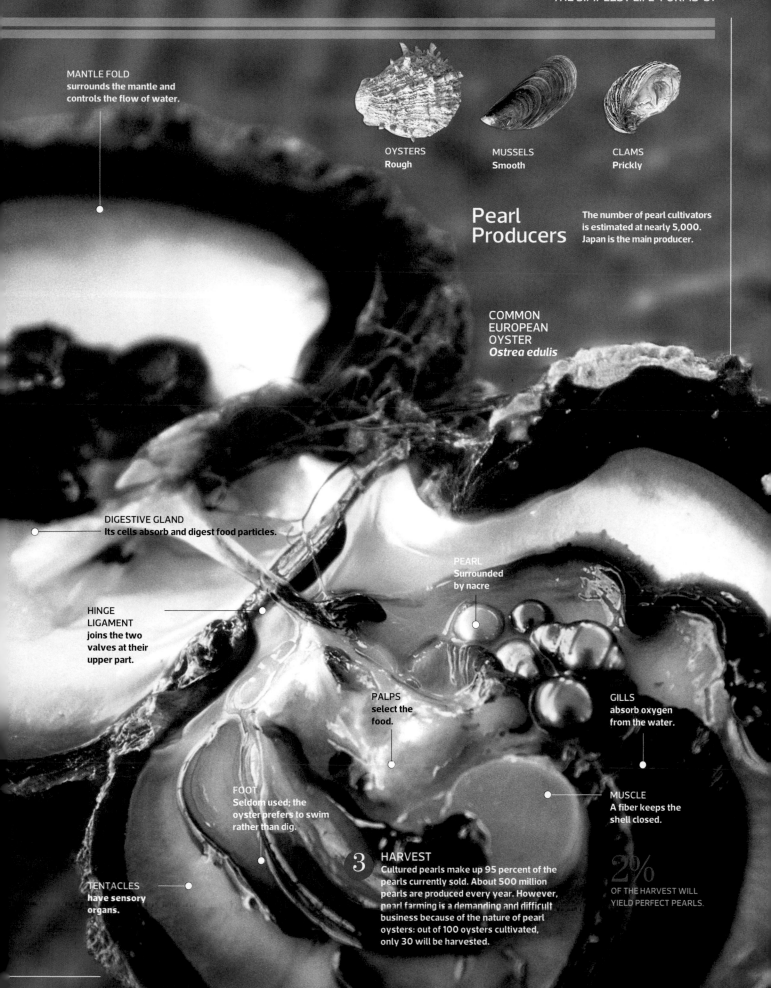

MANTLE FOLD
surrounds the mantle and
controls the flow of water.

OYSTERS
Rough

MUSSELS
Smooth

CLAMS
Prickly

Pearl Producers

The number of pearl cultivators
is estimated at nearly 5,000.
Japan is the main producer.

**COMMON
EUROPEAN
OYSTER**
Ostrea edulis

DIGESTIVE GLAND
Its cells absorb and digest food particles.

PEARL
Surrounded
by nacre

**HINGE
LIGAMENT**
joins the two
valves at their
upper part.

PALPS
select the
food.

GILLS
absorb oxygen
from the water.

FOOT
Seldom used; the
oyster prefers to swim
rather than dig.

MUSCLE
A fiber keeps the
shell closed.

3 HARVEST
Cultured pearls make up 95 percent of the
pearls currently sold. About 500 million
pearls are produced every year. However,
pearl farming is a demanding and difficult
business because of the nature of pearl
oysters: out of 100 oysters cultivated,
only 30 will be harvested.

2%
OF THE HARVEST WILL
YIELD PERFECT PEARLS.

TENTACLES
have sensory
organs.

Powerful Tentacles

The eight-tentacled octopus is one of the few large ocean cephalopods to live in deep water. It is usually found on the rocky or sandy bottoms of shallow waters near the mouths of rivers. It generally moves slowly, sometimes moving in brief spurts, but it can reach great speeds when hunting or fleeing. Some are quite intelligent, having highly evolved brains. ●

Masters of Color

For the octopus, taking on the color of the ocean floor is a camouflage strategy to hide from its prey. In deeper waters, another tactic is to become luminescent to attract the prey. But when the octopus changes colors while doing a certain dance, it is trying to attract the opposite sex.

4 miles per hour
(6 km/h)

Maximum speed of a fleeing octopus. Its speed is comparable to that of a fast-walking human.

SKIN
The skin is a highly elastic membrane that completely covers the octopus.

HEAD
The head compresses and expands, depending on the octopus's breathing and movements. The head contains the brain but without a rigid protective structure.

Attack

➤ To attack, the octopus points its funnel in the direction opposite to its motion. The common octopus (*Octopus vulgaris*), a species that can grow up to 40 inches (1 m) long and inhabits the Mediterranean Sea and North Atlantic Ocean, moves among the rocks on the seafloor, preferably at night. It surprises its prey and makes skillful use of its tentacles and jaws, which can rotate.

The funnel muscles can act as a mechanism for fleeing. Rather than directing the funnel forward, though, the octopus directs it to advance toward its prey.

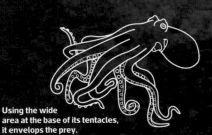

The tentacles stretch forward and outward as the octopus advances.

Using the wide area at the base of its tentacles, it envelops the prey.

Large Predators

Depending on its size, an octopus (like other large cephalopods such as the nautilus, cuttlefish, and squid) is carnivorous and eats both fish and other invertebrates: mollusks and crustaceans, especially crabs. It secretes a venom with its saliva to finish killing the prey before swallowing it.

Speedy Escape

▶ The flow of water into and out of the funnel is regulated by alternately contracting and relaxing ring-shaped muscles and long muscles. By regulating the force at which the water is expelled, the octopus can flee at high speed through a kind of jet propulsion. The octopus moves in the direction its head is pointing, with its tentacles outstretched.

The ring-shaped muscles relax, and the long muscles contract. Water enters.

When the ring-shaped muscles contract, they expel a jet of water that propels the octopus backward.

SELF-DEFENSE WITH INK
A gland located near the anus contracts when the octopus senses danger, expelling a fluid that creates a dark cloud in the water.

TENTACLES
All eight tentacles have the same length. In the male, one tentacle functions as a genital organ.

1 BREATHING

Head

H_2O

2 PROPULSION

Funnel · Gill

The Funnel
The funnel is the exit from the octopus's respiratory cavity. It is also extremely important for the creature's movement. The gills, inside the mantle, absorb oxygen from the water. When the cavity fills, the gills exchange oxygen for carbon dioxide to be emptied from the cavity.

EYES
Are located on the head. The octopus's sense of sight is exceptionally well developed.

MUSCLES
Powerful and versatile, with self-controlled movements, an octopus can move the entire weight of its body.

Grasping Ability

An octopus often crawls among the rocks. Using the system of suckers, or adhesive discs, on its tentacles, an octopus clings to the seafloor or supports itself by attaching the suckers to the surfaces it encounters. By grasping with its forward tentacles, it can drag the rest of its body in that direction.

SUCKERS
Arranged in two rows on the lower surfaces for clinging to rocks and for grasping prey.

1 relaxed muscle

chitinous ring

SUCTION

2 contracted muscle

Crustaceans and Arachnids

Spiders, snakes, ticks, and mites all belong to the same class, Arachnida. They are covered with sensory hairs so tiny that they cannot be seen by the naked eye. In Greek mythology, Arachne was a woman who challenged the goddess Athena to weave faster than she herself could. This angered the goddess, who turned Arachne into a spider, forcing

her to weave forever. That is where these creatures get their name. Within the world of crustaceans, well-known animals such as the shrimp, lobster, and crab are also discussed in this chapter.

You will find details about their anatomy, their differences and similarities, and the way in which they live that will surprise you. Some species breathe through gills and also breathe through their skin. ●

Colorful Armor

E ven though they inhabit all known environments, crustaceans are most closely identified with the aquatic environment. That environment is where they were transformed into arthropods with the most evolutionary success. Their bodies are divided into three parts: the cephalothorax, with antennae and strong mandibles; the abdomen, or pleon; and the back (telson). Some crustaceans are very small: sea lice, for instance, are no larger than one hundredth of an inch (a quarter of a millimeter). The Japanese spider crab, on the other hand, is more than 9 feet (3 m) long with outstretched legs, as it has legs in both the abdomen and the thorax in addition to two pairs of antennae. ●

Wood Louse
(Armadillidium vulgare)

This invertebrate, belonging to the order *Isopoda*, is one of the few terrestrial crustaceans, and it is probably the one best adapted to life outside the water. When it feels threatened, it rolls itself up, leaving only its exoskeleton exposed. Even though it can reproduce and develop away from the water, it breathes through gills. The gills are found in its abdominal appendages and for this reason must be kept at specific humidity levels. That is also why the wood louse seeks dark and humid environments, such as under rocks, on dead or fallen leaves, and in fallen tree trunks.

Extended
animal

EXOSKELETON
Divided into
independent parts

Rolled-up
animal

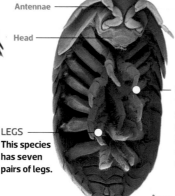

Antennae

Head

LEGS
This species
has seven
pairs of legs.

SEGMENTS
The back segments
are smaller,
and when they
bend, they help
enclose the animal
completely.

Anus

BARNACLE
COLONY

Together Forever

At birth, barnacles *(Pollicipes cornucopia)* are microscopic larvae that travel through the sea until they reach a rocky coast. Then they attach themselves to the shore by means of a stalk, which they develop by the modification of their antennae, and then form a shell. Once they are attached, they remain in one spot for the rest of their lives, absorbing food from the water. Barnacles are edible.

Malacostraca

is the name given to the class of crustaceans that groups crabs together with sea lobsters, shrimp, wood lice, and sea lice. The term comes from Greek, and it means "soft-shelled." Sea and river crabs have 10 legs, and one pair of these legs is modified in a pincer form. Malacostraca are omnivorous and have adapted to a great variety of environments; the number of segments of their exoskeleton can vary from a minimum of 16 to more than 60.

APPENDAGES
consist of a lower region
from which two segmented
branches grow, one internal
(endopod) and the other
external (exopod).

THE PACIFIC SPIDER
CRAB CAN WEIGH UP TO

45 pounds
(20 kg).

BARNACLES
WITHOUT
A SHELL

BARNACLE TRANSVERSAL CUT

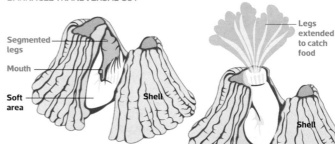

Segmented
legs

Mouth

Soft
area

Shell

Legs
extended
to catch
food

Shell

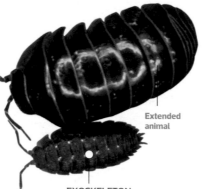

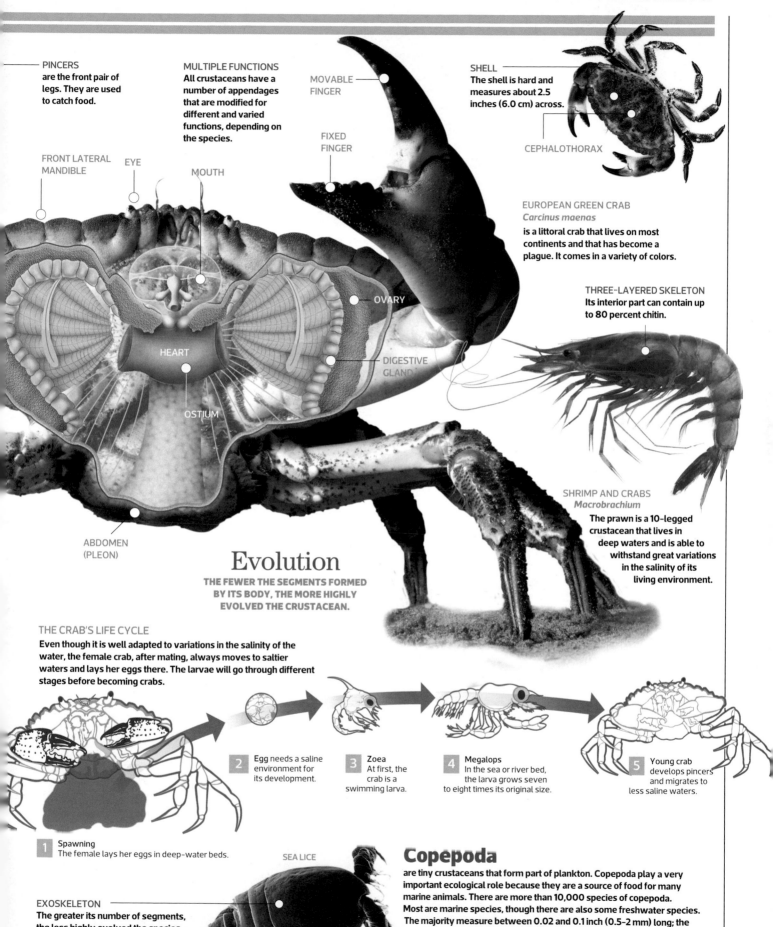

PINCERS
are the front pair of legs. They are used to catch food.

MULTIPLE FUNCTIONS
All crustaceans have a number of appendages that are modified for different and varied functions, depending on the species.

MOVABLE FINGER

FIXED FINGER

FRONT LATERAL MANDIBLE

EYE

MOUTH

OVARY

HEART

DIGESTIVE GLAND

OSTIUM

ABDOMEN (PLEON)

SHELL
The shell is hard and measures about 2.5 inches (6.0 cm) across.

CEPHALOTHORAX

EUROPEAN GREEN CRAB
Carcinus maenas
is a littoral crab that lives on most continents and that has become a plague. It comes in a variety of colors.

THREE-LAYERED SKELETON
Its interior part can contain up to 80 percent chitin.

SHRIMP AND CRABS
Macrobrachium
The prawn is a 10-legged crustacean that lives in deep waters and is able to withstand great variations in the salinity of its living environment.

Evolution

THE FEWER THE SEGMENTS FORMED BY ITS BODY, THE MORE HIGHLY EVOLVED THE CRUSTACEAN.

THE CRAB'S LIFE CYCLE
Even though it is well adapted to variations in the salinity of the water, the female crab, after mating, always moves to saltier waters and lays her eggs there. The larvae will go through different stages before becoming crabs.

1 Spawning
The female lays her eggs in deep-water beds.

2 Egg needs a saline environment for its development.

3 Zoea
At first, the crab is a swimming larva.

4 Megalops
In the sea or river bed, the larva grows seven to eight times its original size.

5 Young crab develops pincers and migrates to less saline waters.

SEA LICE

EXOSKELETON
The greater its number of segments, the less highly evolved the species.

Copepoda

are tiny crustaceans that form part of plankton. Copepoda play a very important ecological role because they are a source of food for many marine animals. There are more than 10,000 species of copepoda. Most are marine species, though there are also some freshwater species. The majority measure between 0.02 and 0.1 inch (0.5-2 mm) long; the smallest ones (*Sphaeronellopsis monothrix*) reach only 0.004 inch (0.11 mm) in length, and the largest (*Pennella balaenopterae*) are 13 inches (32 cm) long.

Changing Outfits

The lobster belongs to the crustaceans, which are characterized by, among other things, an exoskeleton that supports and protects the body of the animal. The exoskeleton has both advantages and disadvantages. The stiffness of the structure prevents growth, which is why the animal grows only when the shell is renewed. This process is called molting. During molting the layers of the new cuticle harden, and minerals and materials from the old exoskeleton are reabsorbed to create a new exoskeleton. ●

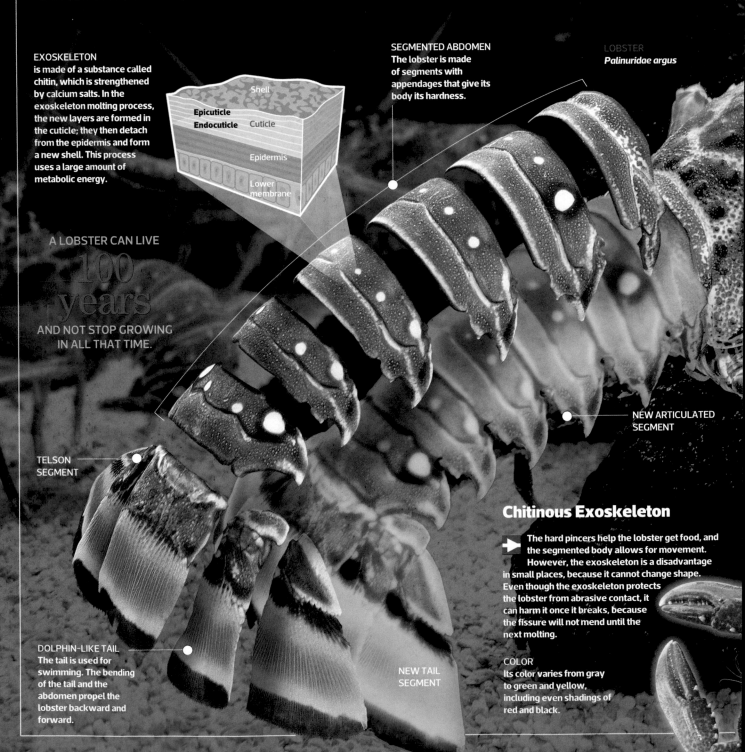

EXOSKELETON
is made of a substance called chitin, which is strengthened by calcium salts. In the exoskeleton molting process, the new layers are formed in the cuticle; they then detach from the epidermis and form a new shell. This process uses a large amount of metabolic energy.

Shell
Epicuticle
Endocuticle   Cuticle
Epidermis
Lower membrane

SEGMENTED ABDOMEN
The lobster is made of segments with appendages that give its body its hardness.

LOBSTER
Palinuridae argus

A LOBSTER CAN LIVE
100 years
AND NOT STOP GROWING
IN ALL THAT TIME.

NEW ARTICULATED SEGMENT

TELSON SEGMENT

Chitinous Exoskeleton

The hard pincers help the lobster get food, and the segmented body allows for movement. However, the exoskeleton is a disadvantage in small places, because it cannot change shape. Even though the exoskeleton protects the lobster from abrasive contact, it can harm it once it breaks, because the fissure will not mend until the next molting.

DOLPHIN-LIKE TAIL
The tail is used for swimming. The bending of the tail and the abdomen propel the lobster backward and forward.

NEW TAIL SEGMENT

COLOR
Its color varies from gray to green and yellow, including even shadings of red and black.

Molting of the Exoskeleton

The presence of the stiff exoskeleton means that crustacean growth takes place during the molting cycle. This phenomenon occurs cyclically and frequently in the young of the species, with longer periods between molts as the crab matures. During ecdysis (when the crab molts), the old shell breaks and detaches, and the animal is helpless. Many functions, such as reproduction, behavior, and metabolic processes are directly affected by the physiology of the molt.

CEPHALOTHORAX is formed by the abdomen and the fused segments of the head and the thorax, all of which are covered by the shell.

MOVABLE EYE

ANTENNULE

ANTENNAE

PINCER-SHAPED LEG

WALKING LEGS Five pairs of legs, of which one or more pairs are modified into pincers.

FROM THE BURSTING OF THE FIRST SKELETON

1 Once the crab reaches adulthood, its exoskeleton covers its body without any change for about 300 days.

2 Between 30 and 40 days before ecdysis, new bristles form, and the epidermis detaches itself.

3 Hours before the break, the lobster takes in large quantities of water until it fills up and breaks the old exoskeleton.

4 During ecdysis itself, the lobster remains immobile for approximately 12 hours, while it grows in size because of hydration.

VULNERABLE While it waits for the new exoskeleton to grow, the lobster hides so it does not end up a victim of its predators.

THE LOBSTER MOLTS **once a year.**

HERMIT CRAB *Dardanus arrosor*

In a Stranger's Home

Hermit crabs belong to the Paguridae and Coenobitidae families. Unlike other crustaceans, a hermit crab does not have a hard exoskeleton on its abdomen to protect it. This is why it uses shells from sea snails as protection for part of its body.

Sharp Front Legs

Crustaceans have appendages that generally branch in two directions and are adapted to aquatic life. A characteristic shared by all crustaceans is their articulated shell, which leaves two pairs of antennae uncovered. They also have a pair of mandibles, two pairs of maxillae, and a pair of appendages in each segment of the body. Their pincers have enough strength so they can trap their prey and feed themselves. The class Malacostraca includes lobsters, crabs, shrimp, and prawns, among other animals. ●

Shrimp

is the name for about 2,000 species of crustaceans of the suborder Natantia. Shrimp are characterized by their semitransparent and flat bodies, with appendages modified for swimming, and by their long antennae. Their length varies between 0.1 inch and about 8 inches (from a few mm to 20 cm), depending on the species. They live in salt water, brackish water, and fresh water. They survive by burying themselves for almost the entire day and coming out at dusk to catch their food.

PRAWN
Caridea

ABDOMEN

55,000
LIVING SPECIES AND AS MANY FOSSIL SPECIES ARE PART OF THIS GROUP OF INVERTEBRATES.

CARAPACE

ANTENNAE
The brain receives the information sent by the antennae and communicates with the rest of the body through the ventral nerve.

TELSON
Fin-like structures used for swimming. The telson makes up the caudal fan together with the last abdominal segment and the uropods. There are no appendages.

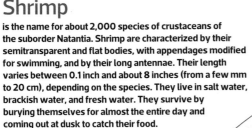

PLEOPODS

FRONT VIEW

UROPODS
are shaped like a spade. The telson is like a barb. Both are used by the shrimp for its characteristic escape backwards.

PEREIOPODS
Five pairs of appendages

FIRST THREE PAIRS
are used to feed itself. The pincers catch and hold prey.

LAST TWO PAIRS
work as walking legs that are aided by the pleopods.

PLEOPODS
First five pairs of abdominal appendages

FIRST TWO PAIRS
have been adapted for sexual functions.

LAST THREE PAIRS
are similar to each other and are used to swim.

Lobster

A lobster is characterized by two enormous pincers formed by the first pair of legs. It lives on rocky bottoms in shallow water, and it migrates seasonally toward the coast in summer and to greater depths in winter. The lobster is typically a nocturnal animal seeking its food when the Sun sets. Its food consists mainly of mollusks, bivalves, worms, and fish.

Crab

Of all crustaceans, the crab has surprising mobility and agility. It has five pairs of legs, four of which are walking legs, despite the fact that it moves laterally instead of forward. The crab-like movement is due to the placement of its legs and the general design of its body. A crab's walk is funny, but its technique is effective for both swimming and walking, even over such varied surfaces as beach sand, rock, and—for some species—tree branches.

AT REST
The body remains close to the ground, the center of gravity is lowered, and movements are slow and rhythmic.

PENDULUM
SLOW WALK
The body operates like the weight of a pendulum. Close to the ground, it saves energy by moving in a swinging motion.

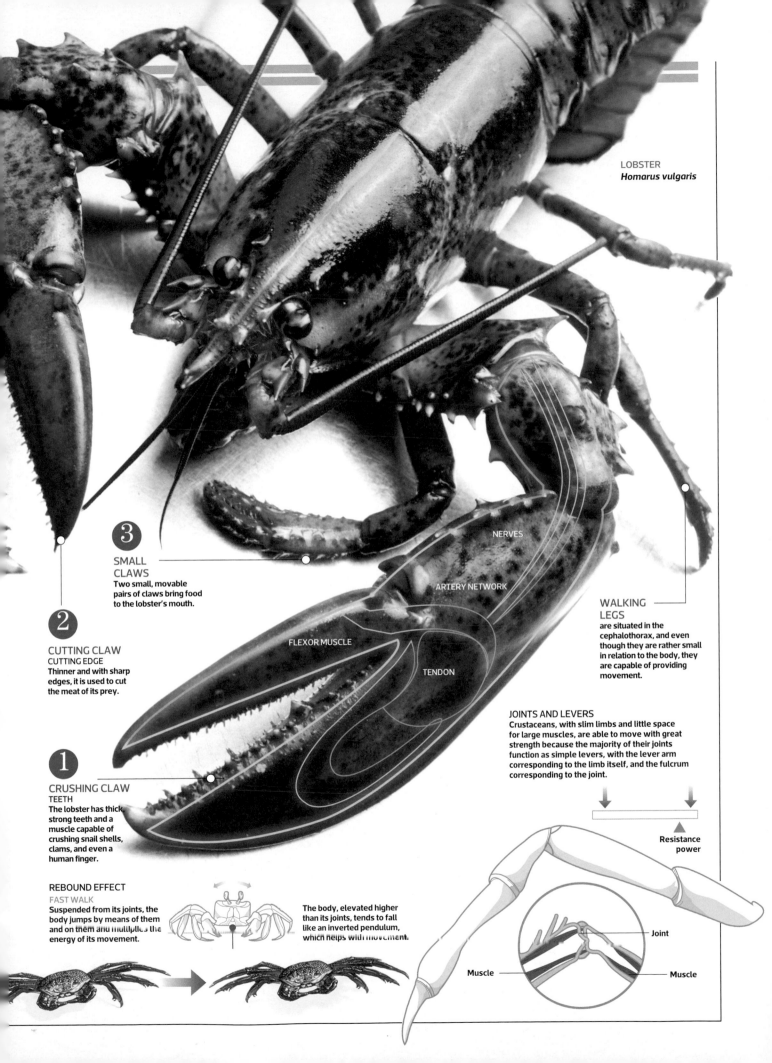

LOBSTER
Homarus vulgaris

NERVES

ARTERY NETWORK

FLEXOR MUSCLE

TENDON

③ SMALL CLAWS
Two small, movable pairs of claws bring food to the lobster's mouth.

② CUTTING CLAW
CUTTING EDGE
Thinner and with sharp edges, it is used to cut the meat of its prey.

① CRUSHING CLAW
TEETH
The lobster has thick, strong teeth and a muscle capable of crushing snail shells, clams, and even a human finger.

WALKING LEGS
are situated in the cephalothorax, and even though they are rather small in relation to the body, they are capable of providing movement.

JOINTS AND LEVERS
Crustaceans, with slim limbs and little space for large muscles, are able to move with great strength because the majority of their joints function as simple levers, with the lever arm corresponding to the limb itself, and the fulcrum corresponding to the joint.

Resistance power

REBOUND EFFECT
FAST WALK
Suspended from its joints, the body jumps by means of them and on them and multiplies the energy of its movement.

The body, elevated higher than its joints, tends to fall like an inverted pendulum, which helps with movement.

Joint

Muscle

Muscle

In the Middle of the Chain

ooplankton include thousands of distinct species belonging to very different groups. Among these species are protists, coelenterates, worms, crustaceans, and other small, weakly swimming organisms. Unicellular, eukaryotic protists constitute a large group of species of zooplankton. They constitute an extensive and varied community in the food network. The phytoplankton, which are capable of photosynthesis, provide food for the zooplankton. Phytoplankton also serve as food for echinoderms, crustaceans, and larval-stage fish. Once they grow up, the larvae serve as food for schools of small fish, which are in turn food for larger fish, including plankton-feeding whales that sometimes eat these small fish.

Malacostraca

Are typically oceanic, though some have adapted to fresh water, and others are even adapted to life on land. All have a body divided into a 13-segment cephalothorax with 13 pairs of appendages, a stomach with six segments, and, at the extreme posterior, an unsegmented telson.

KRILL
Euphausia superba

Is one of the most abundant and successful species on the Earth. Krill can live 5 to 10 years, experiencing 10 moltings before reaching their maximum length. Krill typically emit a greenish light that can be seen at night.

REAL SIZE
1.5 inches
(3.8 cm)

EYE
Krill have only one large, compound, black eye.

6,600 feet
(2,000 m)

DEPTH TO WHICH SWARMS OF KRILL MAY GATHER

LEGS
With their feathery legs krill filter out the small algae on which they feed.

HOW IT FLEES

The krill makes use of its telson, comprising five paddles, to drive itself through the water. It reaches great speed and moves jumping forward and backward. These crustaceans group in giant schools, with thousands of individuals concentrated in each cubic yard of water.

0 second

0.5 second

1 second

10 inches
(25 cm)

20 inches
(50 cm)

TROPHIC CHAIN

The food cycle is initiated with a vegetable producer, which begins the chain for consumers. Those that feed on producers are primary consumers, those that feed on primary consumers are secondary consumers, and so on.

Tertiary consumers — 10 — Right Whale

Secondary consumers — 100 — Octopuses, penguins, fish

Primary consumers — 1,000 — Zooplankton

— 10,000 —

Producers — Phytoplankton

LUMINESCENCE
Each specimen of krill has a photophore in its abdomen, a structure that allows it to emit light because of a chemical reaction that involves oxygen and various other chemical compounds called luciferin, luciferase, and adenosine triphosphate (ATP). One order of crustaceans is generically known as krill.

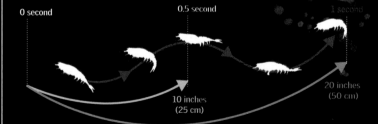

12,000
SPECIES OF COPEPODS

Copepods

are aquatic microcrustaceans, though terrestrial ones also exist. They are found in fresh water as well as in salt water. They feed on phytoplankton and are an important component of plankton, which at the same time serves as food for numerous marine animals.

LARGE APPENDAGES
They form very fine combs that filter the water for food.

REAL SIZE

—
0.08 inch (2 mm)

CYCLOPOID COPEPOD
Megacyclops viridis

Cyclopoid copepod larvae are luminescent. After their developmental stage they begin to swim freely. The cyclopoid copepod lives in fresh water. It is among the most numerous invertebrate species found in Europe.

NAUPLIUS LARVA
Cyclops

This little crustacean swims by jumping with its legs. It feeds on animal and plant remains.

FEET
attract the water current toward the larva's mouth, which little particles can enter.

Branchiopods

are the most primitive types of crustaceans. They live in lakes and ponds throughout the world. They have compound eyes and usually a protective plate, or carapace. They also have many body segments.

WATER FLEA
Daphnia

has two pairs of antennae and feet adapted to swimming and grasping. The second antenna pair serves as a locomotive organ. The water flea feeds on microscopic seaweed and the remains of dead animals.

REAL SIZE

—
0.1 inch (3 mm)

6 to 8 weeks
IS THE AVERAGE LIFESPAN OF A WATER FLEA.

A Special Family

Arachnids make up the largest and most important class of chelicerata. Among them are spiders, scorpions, fleas, ticks, and mites. Arachnids were the first arthropods to colonize terrestrial environments. The fossil remains of scorpions are found beginning in the Silurian Period, and they show that these animals have not undergone major changes in their morphology and behavior. The most well-known arachnids are the scorpions and spiders.●

GIANT HOUSEHOLD SPIDER
Tegenaria duellica

This spider is distinguished by its long legs in relation to its body.

The female can transport up to 30 offspring on its back.

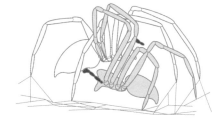

PEDIPALPS
The terminal pedipalp forms a copulating organ through which the male inseminates the female.

PEDIPALPS
act as sensory organs and manipulate food. Males also use them for copulation.

Scorpions

Feared by people for ages, the scorpion is characterized by the fact that its chelicerae (mouth parts that in scorpions are large) and pedipalps form a pincer. The body is covered with a chitinous exoskeleton that includes the cephalothorax and abdomen.

EMPEROR SCORPION
Pandinus imperator
Like other scorpions, it has a stinger crisscrossed by venomous glands. It measures between 5 and 7 inches (12 and 18 cm) long, though some have reached a length of 8 inches (20 cm).

The claws hold the prey and immobilize it.

CHELICERAE
move up and down. In the more primitive spiders (such as tarantulas), the chelicerae move side to side like a pincer.

Saliva glands

Tick

Middle stomach

Palps

Visible dorsal capitulum with dorsal projections that can be removed easily from the tick.

Adhesion material

Infection

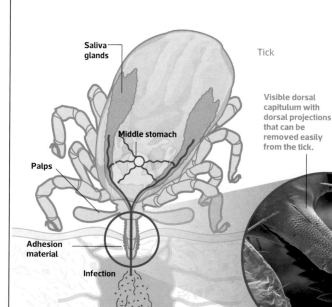

Mites and Ticks

Both are members of the Acari order. They are differentiated by their size. Mites are smaller; ticks may measure up to an inch in length (several centimeters). Mites have many diverse forms and are parasites of animals and plants. Ticks have a common life cycle of three stages: larva, nymph, and adult, during which they live off the blood of their hosts.

Tick   Palps

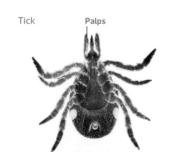

Mite   Palps

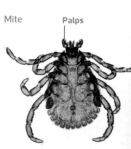

100,000
IS THE NUMBER OF SPECIES OF ARACHNIDS THOUGHT TO EXIST IN THE WORLD.

EXOSKELETON
Growth happens through molting, a process by which the spider gets rid of its old exoskeleton. In its youth the spider grows through successive moltings (up to four a year), and once it reaches adulthood, it goes through a yearly change.

1 The front edge of the shell comes off, and the tegument separates from the abdomen.

2 The spider raises and lowers its legs until the skin slips and falls.

3 It removes the old exoskeleton, and the new one hardens on contact with the air.

CEPHALOTHORAX (PROSOMA)

ABDOMEN (OPISTHOSOMA)

CHELICERAE

SIMPLE EYE

HEART

CLOACA

INTESTINE

OVARIES

LUNG

VENOM GLAND

STOMACH

GENITAL ORIFICE

SILK GLAND

FEMUR

PATELLA

TIBIA

WALKING LEGS
The spider has four pairs of legs for walking. The hairs help it to recognize terrain.

METATARSUS

TARSUS

WITH ITS LEGS SPREAD OUT, A SPIDER CAN MEASURE

12 inches
(30 cm)
IN LENGTH.

Spiders
are the most common arthropods. They have the surprising property of secreting a substance that, on contact with the air, creates very fine threads that spiders skillfully manage for diverse purposes. Once a female spider mates, she deposits her eggs inside a cocoon of special silk, called an egg sack. The appearance of spiders is unmistakable: the two main sections of the body, the thorax (also called a prosoma) and the abdomen (also called an opisthosoma), are united by a narrow stalk (the pedicel). Spiders have four pairs of eyes, whose distinctive size and placement help characterize different families of spiders. Their chelicerae end in fangs that carry conduits from venom glands. Spiders kill their prey by using their chelicerae to apply venom.

Amblypygi
Small arachnids measure between 0.2 and 2 inches (0.4 and 4.5 cm). The chelicerae are not as large, though the pedipalps are strong and are used to capture prey. The first pair of legs are modified touch-and-sensing appendages, whereas the last three take care of movement. Because of a spider's flattened body, its walk is similar to that of the crab.

PEDIPALP
ARACHNID
Phryna grossetaitai

Quality Silk

Spiders are known for the production of silk, with which they construct spiderwebs. With the threads made in their glands, spiders can capture prey, defend themselves, or care for their offspring. Seven types of silk-secreting glands are known, but no spider has all seven types at one time. Inside the gland, the silk that spiders produce is liquid, though it emerges as a solid fiber.●

Threads of Silk

The silk thread made by spiders is produced in two or three pairs of spinnerets that contain hundreds of microscopic tubes that lead to the abdominal silk-producing glands. The thread emerges as a liquid that hardens upon being secreted by the spinnerets. These masters of weaving produce many threads at once. When secreting the silk substance, a scleroprotein, spiders cover it with a thin, fatty layer. Scientists believe that some spiderwebs imitate the ultraviolet images of flowers. Such imitation lures many butterflies and bees to fall into the spider's sticky trap.

COMPOSITION
The silk is made of complex proteins. Males as well as females generally have five to seven different types of special silk glands for producing these proteins.

SPINNERETS
The silk emerges through spinnerets; the thin threads are joined to each other before they dry to form a thicker strand.

SILK GLAND
Moves the silk to the spinnerets. The secretion is a liquid substance that is insoluble in water.

30%
The amount that a thread of silk can stretch from its original length

Diverse Uses of Thread

In addition to spiderwebs, traps, and shelter lining, spider silk has other uses. The spider can use it as a thread for tracking its position or as a safety thread when it either lowers itself or is suddenly dislodged and falling. A spider can also use the silk thread to suspend itself in midair. Male spiders use silk as a web where they deposit their sperm before leaving in search of a female, who uses the silk to build egg sacks, where she will deposit her eggs.

LINING

SPERM

EGG SACK

SECURITY

FABRICATION

WEB

Architecture

The appearance of a spiderweb depends on the spider that wove it. There are very well-designed structures, such as the hammock web built under bushes by the tiny *Linyphia triangularis*. Other webs, such as those of the families Linyphiidae and Agelenidae, are not made of sticky silk but only a dry variety. The silk of the spider is almost as strong as steel, and it has double the elasticity of nylon. Some giant tropical spiders build spiderwebs that are as strong as fishing nets, with which they can trap even birds.

5 REPLACEMENT
Dry web material breaks from the action of the chelicerae and from food trapped in the web. The spider replaces this broken material with stickier and thicker silk.

4 RADIUS
With the silk glands (glandulae ampullaceae), the spider constructs the spokes of the web. Dry strands that run from one spoke to the next form a spiral.

3 SUPPORT
The spider creates the support structure that it will attach to a nearby object. This object might be a tree trunk, a wall, or a rock.

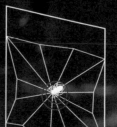

2 TRIANGLES
The spider adds a loose thread fastened to each side of the bridge, moves to the middle of the bridge, and lowers itself to form a triangle with the silk.

1 BEGINNING
The threads set up a bridge. The spider lets itself sway in the wind until it falls and finds its footing.

2,500
THE NUMBER OF RECORDED SPECIES OF WEB-SPINNING SPIDERS

Sixth Sense

Spiders do not have good vision and can see only a short distance. For this reason, they carry out many of their activities at night. However, some spiders do have sharp vision. To be aware of the world around them, spiders use the sensory hairs that are located at the ends of their limbs. Each body hair is sensitive to differences in pressure. Some hairs are also capable of transmitting vibrations to the exoskeleton.

Hairs

Are used to conduct stimuli to the cells. Some are short and stiff, others long and flexible. According to the form of the hair, the mechanoreceptors provide the spider with information about the world that surrounds it. The stimuli induce the animal to flee from enemies, obtain food, and establish the reflexes needed to walk, run, fight, or mate.

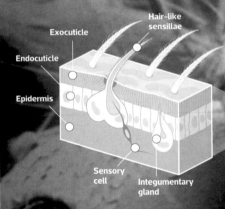

Exocuticle
Endocuticle
Epidermis
Hair-like sensillae
Sensory cell
Integumentary gland

Sensillae

TRICHOBOTHRIA is a long, tactile hair.

TACTILE HAIR perceives the sensory flow of the environment.

Sensillae

Action Contact with the air

Action Contact with an object

Hairs that feel vibrations and sense the presence of strangers

Reaction The hair does not bend, and the angle decreases.

Reaction The hair curves, and the angle is greater.

Trichobothria perceives movements.

EYELET
Allows for
360-degree vision.

EYE
The retina inside the
eye can move in three
dimensions, which
permits the spider to
look in all directions and
focus on an object.

Chelicerae and Eyes

Chelicerae are formed by two segments: a
basal segment that contains the venom gland
and the rest of the appendage that forms a
fang at the end of which the venom channel opens.
Normally spiders have eight simple eyes, each one
supplied with a single lens, optical rods, and a retina.
The eyes are basically used for the perception of
moving objects, but some can form images.

OGREFACED
SPIDER
Dinopis
Two powerful eyes

JUMPING SPIDER
Phidippus audax
Four large eyes on the
front of its head and four
smaller eyes on the upper
part of the head.

DYSDERA CROCOTA
Dysdera
Six small eyes

CRAB SPIDER
Xysticus cristatus
Eight spread-out eyes

Pedipalps: Various Functions

The pedipalps consist of six segments and have
pincers; they are tactile along almost all of their
length, and in the males the ends are modified
to form a receptacle that transfers the sperm during
copulation. The lower parts of the pedipalps are used for
chewing.

TIBIA

THORN

TARSUS

CHELICERAE
Appendage with
a fang that
secretes venom

PEDIPALP
Appendage used
to get to know the
environment

TUFT OF HAIR OF
A CLAW

HAIR (TARSAL
ORGAN)
Senses
humidity

Poisonous Sting

Venomous arachnids are the group of arthropods most feared by people. Even if a bite may be fatal to another animal, it is unlikely that it will be fatal to a human being, who would be attacked only as a means of defense in cases of fear or danger. The scorpion stands out among the most dangerous species. It uses its stinger when it wants to be certain of catching a difficult prey. Another notable example is the black widow, whose tiny body produces one third as much venom as a rattlesnake. ●

The Most Dangerous

Of the 38,000 known species of spiders, only about 30 have venom that is harmful to humans. Some are hunters or trappers, but others are small, peaceful weavers. The black widow (*Latrodectus mactans*) is one of the shyest. The venom that it injects (toxalbumin) is a neurotoxin that acts principally on the nerve endings. Still, the black widow bites only when provoked. The wandering spider (*Phoneutria fera*) is one of the most aggressive arachnids. It is large, and its venom is fast-acting, capable of killing most prey in 15 minutes.

30 species

of spiders have truly dangerous venom.

1 DETECTS THE PREY

The scorpion does not go out in search of food; rather, it waits until food passes by it. The scorpion can also find food by accident.

2 CLOSES IN

The scorpion directs the front of its body toward the animal, approaching to a distance of 2 to 4 inches (5 to 10 cm), when it lowers its pedipalps in preparation for attack.

PALP OR PEDIPALP

CHELICERAE
Because the hunting spider does not have a jaw, it has to use its chelicerae to take its food apart when it feeds. The chelicerae are also used during copulation.

HUNTING SPIDER
Heteropoda venatoria

COMPOSITION
OF VENOM
Spider venom is a cocktail of substances, particularly potassium salts, digestive enzymes, and polypeptides. The potassium alters the electrical balance in the nerves and paralyzes the victim. The peptides disable the cardiac muscles and can also attack the nervous system or cause pulmonary edema.

HOW THE STINGER WORKS

Two conduits run from the venom glands to openings at the end of the telson. When the scorpion stings, muscles press the walls of the telson against the venom glands to force venom through the hole of the stinger into a wound. This process is controlled by the scorpion, which administers the proper dose of venom, since it cannot quickly regenerate the venom if it fails.

TELSON
STINGER
Is located in the last segment.

METASOMA
TAIL

VENOM GLANDS
The secretion comes out through conduits that open near the tip of the stinger.

MUSCLES

DESERT SCORPION
Hadrurus arizonensis

SCORPIONS

Scorpions are grouped in six families, the most important being the Buthidae because it contains the most dangerous species for the potency of their venom. The flat form of their bodies helps them hide under rocks, tree bark, and various kinds of debris. Scorpions have nocturnal habits. Cannibalism is common among scorpions, especially after copulation. The only places in the world where there are no scorpions are Antarctica and Greenland.

OPISTHOSOMA
ABDOMEN

PROSOMA
CEPHALOTHORAX

CENTRAL EYE

PECTEN
This structure is made up of numerous sensory structures, mechanoreceptors, and chemoreceptors.

Conduct of Capture and Sting

Scorpions have long, fine hairs called trichobothria, located in the pedipalps. These perceive the vibration and movement of the wind and help the scorpion detect flying prey and predators. These organs help the scorpion get out of harm's way when danger threatens.

3 ATTACK
Once the scorpion is close to its prey, it walks around the victim, trapping it. Then it uses its pedipalps to contain the attacked animal.

PEDIPALP

CLAW

4 USE OF THE STINGER
If the prey resists, the scorpion uses its stinger to inject the venom. Venom is administered by the scorpion until it kills the animal.

Insects

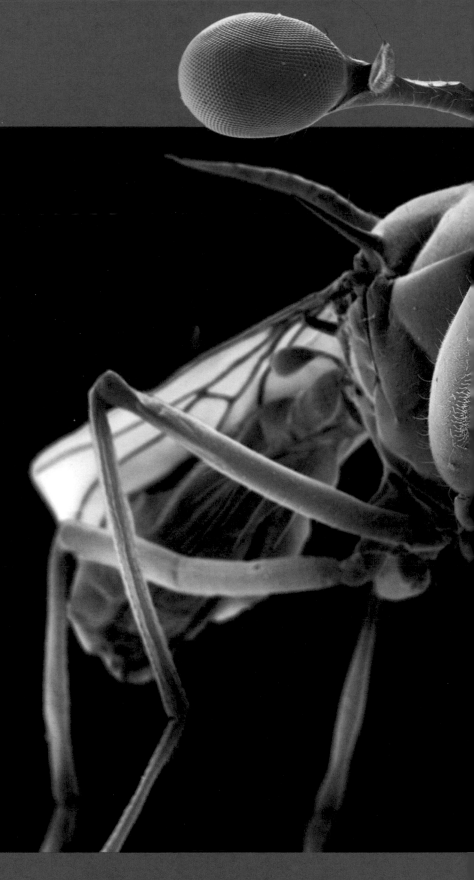

nsects make up the largest and most varied group of arthropods. Most reproduce easily, and there are insects adapted to any environment. Their bodies are protected by a form of armor. Arthropods are currently believe to be the only living things capable of surviving a nuclear winter. They have highly developed sensory organs that enable them to see long distances.

A PECULIAR SENSE OF SIGHT
This tropical insect has a pair
of eyes on each side of its body,
giving it a very wide field
of vision.

e diversity and sheer number of
sect species, estimated at 1.5 million,
e a testimony to their evolutionary
ccess. They have been successful, in
rt, because they are small, need less
food than larger organisms, and have
extraordinarily developed means of
movement that keep them from being
easy victims for predators. ●

The Secret of Success

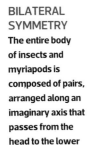 ensory antennae, appendages on the head that can be used to chew, crush, or grab, highly developed eyes on the sides of the head, and pairs of jointed legs with functions that depend on the species—all are outstanding common features of insects and millipedes (subphylum Myriapoda). Insects, also called hexapods, have six legs attached to the thorax. Myriapods are multi-segmented arthropods that have developed only on land. ●

BILATERAL SYMMETRY

The entire body of insects and myriapods is composed of pairs, arranged along an imaginary axis that passes from the head to the lower end of the abdomen.

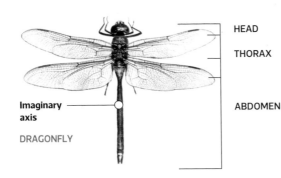

Imaginary axis

DRAGONFLY

HEAD

THORAX

ABDOMEN

Two Pairs of Wings

Some ancient species had three pairs of wings. Today, however, insects have one or two pairs. Butterflies, dragonflies, bees, and wasps use two pairs to fly, but other insects fly with only one pair.

OPEN CIRCULATION

A tubular heart pumps the hemolymph (blood) forward through the dorsal aorta. Accessory contracting organs help push the blood into the wings and legs.

APPENDAGE
contains the genital organs.

SEGMENTED REGIONS
Insects' bodies are divided into three parts: the head (6 segments), the thorax (3 segments), and the abdomen (up to 11 segments).

SPIRACLES
Small entrances to the tracheae

1 million
KNOWN INSECT SPECIES

RESPIRATORY SYSTEM
Land-dwelling arthropods breathe with tracheae. Through branching tubes (tracheoles), air containing oxygen is brought directly to each cell, and carbon dioxide is eliminated.

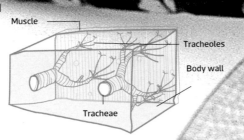

Muscle

Tracheoles

Body wall

Tracheae

Legs Adapted for Each Type of Use

The shape of the arthropod legs shown here is closely related to their use and to the arthropod's habitat. Some species have taste and touch receptors on their legs.

Sacs

STRUCTURE
gives the wings great stability.

LEGS

WALKING
Cockroach

JUMPING
Grasshopper

SWIMMING
Water scorpion

DIGGING
Mole cricket

GATHERING
Bee

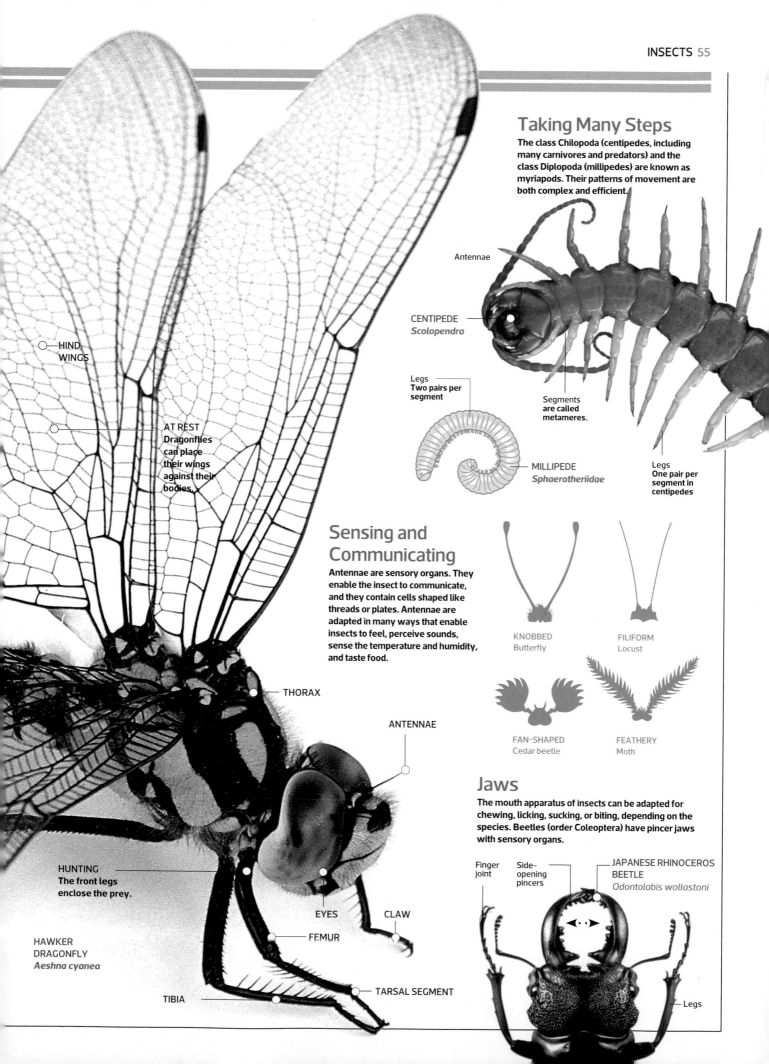

HIND WINGS

AT REST
Dragonflies can place their wings against their bodies.

THORAX

HUNTING
The front legs enclose the prey.

HAWKER DRAGONFLY
Aeshna cyanea

ANTENNAE

EYES

CLAW

FEMUR

TIBIA

TARSAL SEGMENT

Taking Many Steps

The class Chilopoda (centipedes, including many carnivores and predators) and the class Diplopoda (millipedes) are known as myriapods. Their patterns of movement are both complex and efficient.

Antennae

CENTIPEDE
Scolopendra

Legs
Two pairs per segment

Segments are called metameres.

MILLIPEDE
Sphaerotheriidae

Legs
One pair per segment in centipedes

Sensing and Communicating

Antennae are sensory organs. They enable the insect to communicate, and they contain cells shaped like threads or plates. Antennae are adapted in many ways that enable insects to feel, perceive sounds, sense the temperature and humidity, and taste food.

KNOBBED
Butterfly

FILIFORM
Locust

FAN-SHAPED
Cedar beetle

FEATHERY
Moth

Jaws

The mouth apparatus of insects can be adapted for chewing, licking, sucking, or biting, depending on the species. Beetles (order Coleoptera) have pincer jaws with sensory organs.

Finger joint

Side-opening pincers

JAPANESE RHINOCEROS BEETLE
Odontolabis wollastoni

Legs

The Better to See You With

ust as people without color vision have a hard time understanding what color is, it is impossible for humans to imagine what it is like to see through the compound eye of an insect. These eyes are made of thousands of tiny rods called ommatidia, each one a small eye connected directly to the brain. Scientists theorize that the insect's brain composes the images received from each ommatidium, enabling it to perceive movement in any possible direction–in some species, even from behind.

Field of Vision

A fly's ommatidia are arranged in circles, and each one covers a portion of the field of vision. Such systems may not yield a high-resolution image, but they are highly sensitive to movement. The slightest motion causes a transfer of sensitivity from one ommatidium to another. This is what makes it so hard to catch a fly.

FLY
Drosophila

ANTENNA

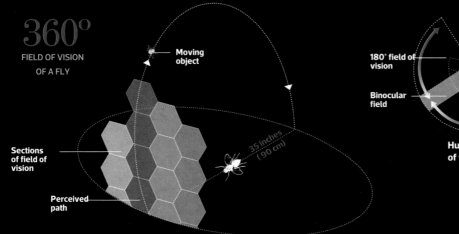

360°
FIELD OF VISION
OF A FLY

Moving
object

Sections
of field of
vision

35 inches
(90 cm)

Perceived
path

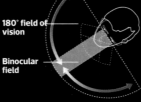

180° field of
vision

Binocular
field

Human field
of vision

MOUTH
The mouth has
apparatus for
licking and
sucking.

A Bee's Eye View

Compared with human vision, a bee's vision is somewhat nearsighted. Even the images of nearby objects are blurry. Its compound eyes have some 6,900 ommatidia.

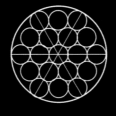

Distorted
midline

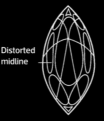

HUMANS
With binocular
vision, a flat and
undistorted image

BEES
In a larger field,
the same image is
narrower.

HEADED FOR NECTAR
Sensitivity to ultraviolet light,
invisible to the human eye,
enables worker bees
to find the nectar inside
the flowers.

Area with
nectar

One Eye, or Thousands

Each ommatidium is responsible for a small portion of the visual field. Depending on the type of light they receive, the pigmented cells around each rhabdom can vary their diameter, regulating the overall sensitivity of the compound eye.

COMPOUND EYE

OMMATIDIUM

ANTENNA

THE HOUSEFLY HAS

4,000

OMMATIDIA

RHABDOM
Connects each lens with its nerve

LENS
Cone-shaped, to direct light to the rhabdom

FLY VISION

Eyelet

Retina

Ommatidia

Antenna

RETINAL CELL

PIGMENT CELL

CORNEA
Hexagonal in shape to fit into the rest of the compound eye

TYPES OF EYES

PROTECTIVE
The eyelets of the tachinid fly cover its eyes.

VISION IN THE ROUND
Certain dragonflies have a completely spherical field of vision.

CALCULATORS This common blue damselfly uses its eyes to calculate distances.

Types of Mouths

F ar from being a mere opening, the mouth is usually one of the most complex parts of an insect's body. The simple oral appendages of the most primitive forms were gradually modified so that this zoological group has been able to expand its diet. Thus, a hunter's mouth is totally different from that of a sucking insect or a leaf-eater, such as the locust. ●

ANTENNA

LOCUST
Family Acrididae
Since ancient times, locusts have been feared as a great plague on crops.

1 day

THE TIME IT TAKES A LOCUST TO EAT ITS OWN WEIGHT IN FOOD

Made to order

➤ The oral appendages of primitive insects were modified considerably, and they took different forms according to the species. The first pair of upper jaws is for holding and sucking the food into the mouth. The second pair of upper jaws fuses at the midline during its development to form the lip, a structure with different functions, depending on the diet. The lower jaws and the first pair of upper jaws are at the side of the mouth, and an upper lip, the labrum, protects the front of the mouth. These parts form the basic biting-chewing apparatus. In more advanced forms, its modifications give rise to structures for sucking and licking or for biting and sucking.

BITING AND CHEWING

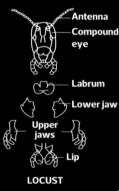

- Antenna
- Compound eye
- Labrum
- Lower jaw
- Upper jaws
- Lip

LOCUST

Strong lower jaws and dexterous upper jaws

PIERCING AND CHEWING

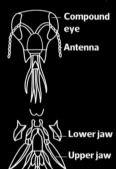

- Compound eye
- Antenna
- Lower jaw
- Upper jaw
- Lip

BEE

Lip for nectar; lower jaws to chew pollen and mold wax

SUCKING

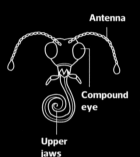

- Antenna
- Compound eye
- Upper jaws

BUTTERFLY

With a small labrum and no lower jaw. The upper jaws form a suction tube.

PUNCTURING AND SUCKING

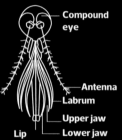

- Compound eye
- Antenna
- Labrum
- Upper jaw
- Lower jaw
- Lip

MOSQUITO (FEMALE)

The lip and upper jaws form a tube; the lower jaws are for puncturing the skin, and the labrum forms a sheath.

SEVEN-SPOT LADYBUG
Coccinella septempunctata feeds on aphids, plant lice, and sand flies.

Leaf Eaters

➤ Insects such as locusts and some beetles, as well as caterpillars (and the larvae of many other species) need a mouth structure capable of cutting leaves into small pieces and then putting them into the mouth. For this purpose their large lower jaws have a series of serrated teeth, whereas the upper jaws and the lip have palps for manipulating and grasping the leaf pieces.

CARNIVORES
use their jaws as pincers to grasp their prey.

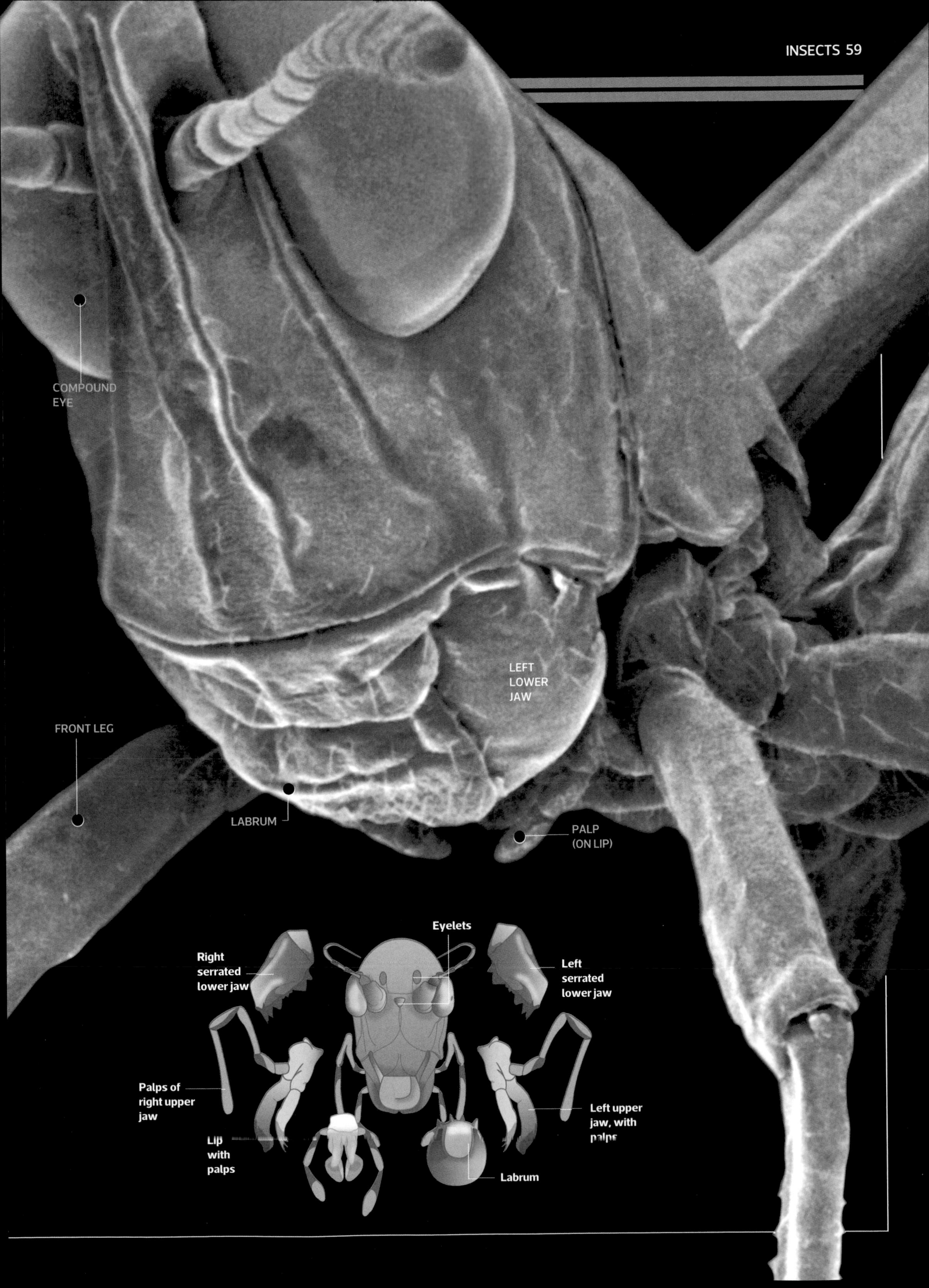

COMPOUND
EYE

FRONT LEG

LEFT
LOWER
JAW

LABRUM

PALP
(ON LIP)

Eyelets

Right
serrated
lower jaw

Left
serrated
lower jaw

Palps of
right upper
jaw

Left upper
jaw, with
palps

Lip
with
palps

Labrum

Sucking and Piercing

Starting with lower jaws adapted for chewing, many insects have developed a more sophisticated oral apparatus, which has enabled them to expand their diet. Mosquitoes, for example, can pierce mammals' skin and feed on their blood using one of the most complex mouths in nature. Flies can eat solid food by using their oral apparatus to begin digestion outside their bodies. Other species have mouths that enable them only to drink liquids. ●

Shapes

PIERCING

SUCKING

Heteroptera (true bug)

Butterfly

Mosquito

Fly

Upper jaw

Tube for nectar

Interlocking bristles

DETAIL CROSS SECTION

The Butterfly

Its upper jaws are modified into a retractable tube. It feeds on accessible fluids, such as nectar.

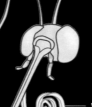

When not in use, the tube is rolled up.

To eat, the insect unfurls the tube.

Epipharynx

Tube for saliva

Tube for food

Lip

Hypopharynx

3 EATING

Once the food is liquefied, the fly sips it up with its proboscis.

The Fly

feeds on soft, damp substances. It uses its mouth to put enzymes onto certain solids to soften them so it can sip them up.

Head of the fly

Eyes

1 WETTING

The fly dampens and softens the food with saliva and digestive juices.

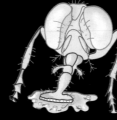

2 MAKING SOUP

These digestive juices break the food down and turn it into a partially digested soup.

LIP
Contains one tube for sucking and another for discharging enzymes

STYLETS
Flexible tool used to pierce and hold in place

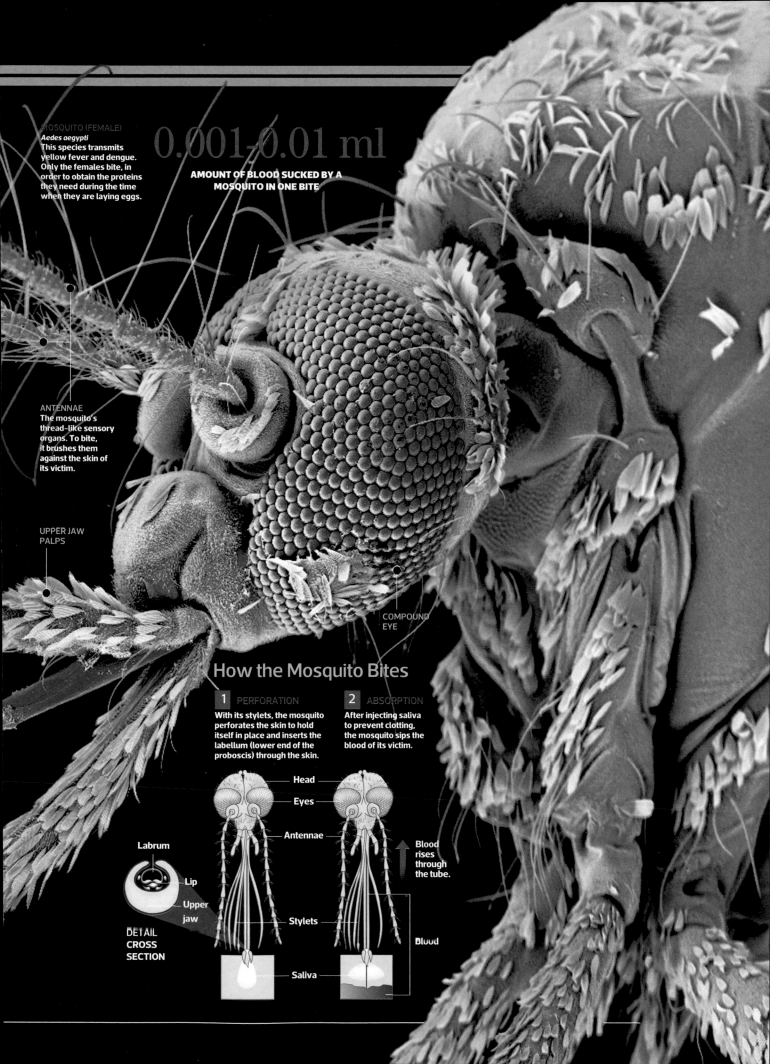

AMOUNT OF BLOOD SUCKED BY A MOSQUITO IN ONE BITE

MOSQUITO (FEMALE)
Aedes aegypti
This species transmits yellow fever and dengue. Only the females bite, in order to obtain the proteins they need during the time when they are laying eggs.

ANTENNAE
The mosquito's thread–like sensory organs. To bite, it brushes them against the skin of its victim.

UPPER JAW PALPS

COMPOUND EYE

How the Mosquito Bites

1 PERFORATION
With its stylets, the mosquito perforates the skin to hold itself in place and inserts the labellum (lower end of the proboscis) through the skin.

2 ABSORPTION
After injecting saliva to prevent clotting, the mosquito sips the blood of its victim.

Head

Eyes

Antennae

Blood rises through the tube.

Labrum

Lip

Upper jaw

Stylets

Blood

DETAIL CROSS SECTION

Saliva

Great Walkers

Etymologically speaking, myriapod means "many feet." The term refers to two very different classes of invertebrates: Class Chilopoda and Class Diplopoda, better known as centipedes and millipedes. All are animals divided into segments. Centipedes, most of which are carnivores, have a pair of legs on each segment, and millipedes have two pairs of legs per segment. These invertebrates (which are not insects) have so many legs that, to walk, they must use a highly sophisticated timing mechanism that seems to follow mathematical principles. ●

Applied Math

To walk, land-dwelling arthropods arch their bodies and move their six legs in coordination so that when one leg moves forward in a power stroke, the ones in front, behind, and opposite it are in a recovery phase, remaining on the ground. Myriapods have a similar mechanism, although it is much more complex because of their large number of legs. The legs are jointed, but they do not function independently of each other for the arthropod to move forward. The segmented body moves side to side in a regular wave pattern, and the legs are functionally adapted to this body movement.

SINUOUS PATH

Not only does an arthropod's body move in wave patterns; when the legs on one side of its body are closest together, those on the other side are farthest apart. This alternating pattern is repeated all along its body.

A CENTIPEDE'S LIFE

Female centipedes lay eggs in the spring and summer. These invertebrates can live up to six years, and it takes them three years to reach maturity.

A Thousand Legs

Millipede, or diplopod, is the name of land-dwelling invertebrate species with multi-segmented bodies that have two pairs of legs on each segment. They live in damp places and feed on decomposing material. All of them have a pair of simple eyes and a pair of antennae, lower jaws, and upper jaws. The largest do not exceed 4 inches (10 cm) in length.

1 LIKE CLAWS

The back legs of this centipede, almost perpendicular to the rest, are used to trap and hold prey while it injects its catch with venom by means of powerful jaws.

SIZE OR QUANTITY

There are species of centipedes that add segments throughout their lives; others are born with a fixed number of segments that grow in size.

Predators

All centipedes are carnivorous and venomous. The largest tropical centipedes can eat worms, insects, and even small birds and mammals.

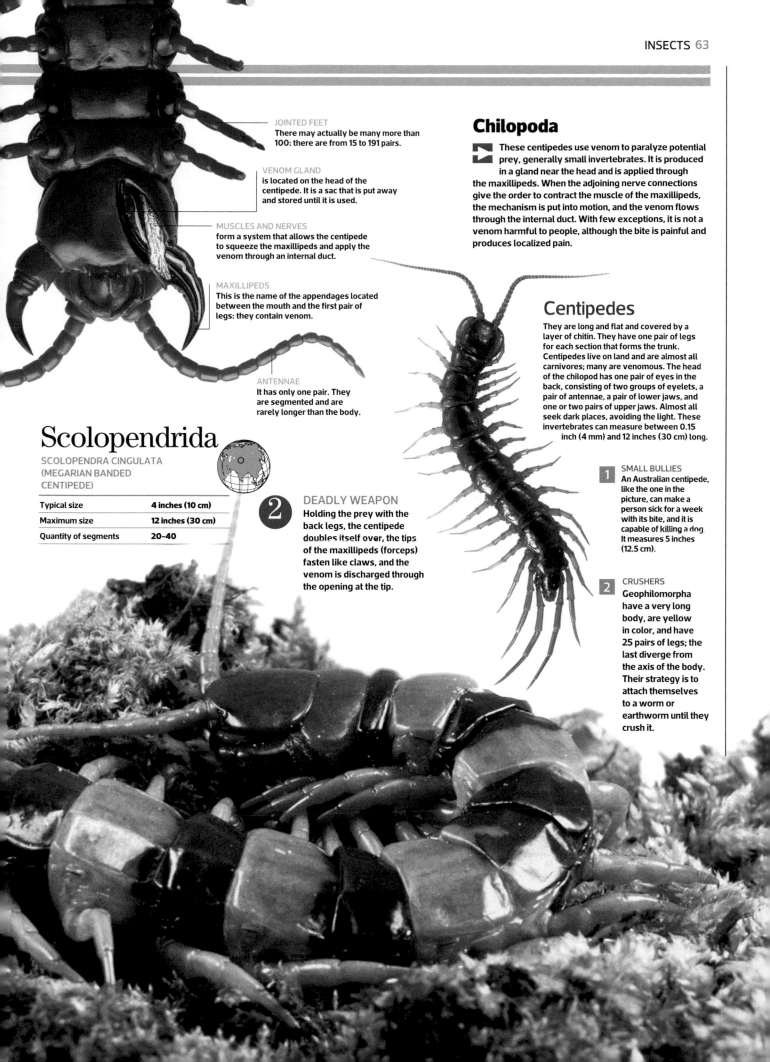

JOINTED FEET
There may actually be many more than 100: there are from 15 to 191 pairs.

VENOM GLAND
is located on the head of the centipede. It is a sac that is put away and stored until it is used.

MUSCLES AND NERVES
form a system that allows the centipede to squeeze the maxillipeds and apply the venom through an internal duct.

MAXILLIPEDS
This is the name of the appendages located between the mouth and the first pair of legs: they contain venom.

ANTENNAE
It has only one pair. They are segmented and are rarely longer than the body.

Chilopoda

These centipedes use venom to paralyze potential prey, generally small invertebrates. It is produced in a gland near the head and is applied through the maxillipeds. When the adjoining nerve connections give the order to contract the muscle of the maxillipeds, the mechanism is put into motion, and the venom flows through the internal duct. With few exceptions, it is not a venom harmful to people, although the bite is painful and produces localized pain.

Centipedes

They are long and flat and covered by a layer of chitin. They have one pair of legs for each section that forms the trunk. Centipedes live on land and are almost all carnivores; many are venomous. The head of the chilopod has one pair of eyes in the back, consisting of two groups of eyelets, a pair of antennae, a pair of lower jaws, and one or two pairs of upper jaws. Almost all seek dark places, avoiding the light. These invertebrates can measure between 0.15 inch (4 mm) and 12 inches (30 cm) long.

1 SMALL BULLIES
An Australian centipede, like the one in the picture, can make a person sick for a week with its bite, and it is capable of killing a dog. It measures 5 inches (12.5 cm).

2 CRUSHERS
Geophilomorpha have a very long body, are yellow in color, and have 25 pairs of legs; the last diverge from the axis of the body. Their strategy is to attach themselves to a worm or earthworm until they crush it.

Scolopendrida

**SCOLOPENDRA CINGULATA
(MEGARIAN BANDED
CENTIPEDE)**

Typical size	4 inches (10 cm)
Maximum size	12 inches (30 cm)
Quantity of segments	20–40

2 DEADLY WEAPON
Holding the prey with the back legs, the centipede doubles itself over, the tips of the maxillipeds (forceps) fasten like claws, and the venom is discharged through the opening at the tip.

High-Quality Jumpers

Fleas are well known for their extraordinary jumps. When they are adults, these small, wingless insects take advantage of their jumping ability to hunt for their food, the blood of birds and mammals. They are ectoparasites of dogs, cats, and chickens, which keeps them present in our daily lives. They invariably bite their hosts and suck the blood that circulates through their skin. ●

FLEAS CAN SURVIVE

3 months

WITHOUT EATING.

Superprotein

The capacity to jump is related to the presence of resilin, a protein of great elasticity similar to rubber. Flea resilin has the function of building tension in the jumping legs. The release of accumulated energy generates the jump. On occasion the jump is useless, and the flea does not manage to place itself on the host. Far from being a failure, the fall adds to the tension of the resilin, which makes the rebound a longer jump.

FLEAS IN THE HOME

Fleas are very common on dogs and cats. Fleabites generate serious discomfort for domestic animals because scratching irritates and injures their skin.

② Action

The flea accumulates energy by tensing the muscles of the thorax and legs. When the accumulated elastic energy reaches a certain level, the flea releases its legs. As a result the legs generate a sudden movement that causes the flea to jump.

JUMPING LEG
The legs are furnished with extra upper segments. These supplements allow it to jump with speed.

Key System

1 The muscles in the coxa contract, generating enormous tension. The resistance to the tension is supported by the exoskeleton.

2 Once the jump is started, within thousandths of a second the direction, intensity, and orientation of the jump are all established by the torque that the muscles and leg segments create for the flea to complete its jump.

① Preparation

Within tenths of a second, the flea prepares itself to jump. It compresses the resilin and at the same time contracts its back legs. The back legs have a system of pads that retain the tension and accumulate energy.

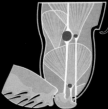

Order of Jumpers

▶ Fleas are in the class Insecta, order Siphonoptera, which includes wingless insects that are external parasites and lack wings. Their mouth apparatus is for piercing and sucking, and their life cycle is one of complete metamorphosis. Their 16 families include the genera of fleas that infest cats and dogs (*Ctenocephalides canis and C. felis*), as well as those that infest hens (*Ceratophyllus gallinae*).

DOG FLEAS
Ctenocephalides canis
This species is responsible for 90 percent of flea infestations in dogs.

HUMAN FLEA
Pulex irritans
usually feeds on human blood. Unlike other fleas, they do not remain on the host.

200 times
THE DISTANCE A FLEA CAN JUMP IN TERMS OF BODY LENGTH

③

In Flight

A flea can leap 24 inches (60 cm) at one bound. Its body is protected by armor-like overlapping plates that make up its exoskeleton. During a series of jumps, fleas can fall on their backs or heads without being injured.

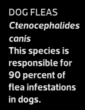

LARVA

EGGS

TOTAL CHANGE
Fleas are holometabolous; that is, their typical lifestyle includes a complete metamorphosis.

PUPA

ADULT FLEA

Life Cycle

▶ A complete cycle, from egg to adult, can take from two to eight months. The length of the cycle varies by species and by temperature, humidity in the environment, and the availability of food. In general, after feeding on blood, the female lays 20 eggs per day and up to 600 eggs throughout her life. The eggs are laid on the host (dogs, cats, rabbits, mice, rats, opossums, humans, etc.).

Edible Blood

▶ As parasites of warm-blooded animals, fleas are classified as hematophagous (blood-eating) insects. Adults suck the blood of their hosts, which contains nutrients that they use for their own nutrition. Females use these nutrients to produce their eggs. The dried blood ejected in the adults' feces is also useful as food for various types of larvae.

1 The front legs are important for feeding. They hold the insect in place as it prepares to bite.

2 On injecting their stylet, fleas expel a substance that irritates the host but helps the fleas by keeping the blood from clotting while they are sucking it.

FLEA VS. MAN
A flea jumps a distance equivalent to 200 times the length of its body. To equal this feat, a man would have to jump over a 130-story building.

The Art of Flying

ne of the most basic adaptations of insects has been their ability to fly. Most have two pairs of wings. Beetles (order Coleoptera) use one pair to fly and one pair for protection. For example, the rounded body of a ladybug or ladybird is nothing more than the covering for a very sophisticated flight system. It makes these small beetles, which are harmless to humans, great hunters in the insect world.

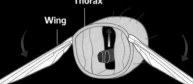

The vertical muscle contracts and the wings move upward.

Thorax

Wing

The horizontal muscle contracts and the wings move downward.

"Ladies" of Land and Air

 Some 4,500 species of these beetles live throughout the world. Almost all are brightly colored, with black spots on a red, yellow, or orange background. These colors warn away predators, who usually associate bright colors with poison. In fact, some ladybugs are actually poisonous for small predators, such as lizards and small birds. Ladybugs pose the greatest danger to agricultural pests such as plant lice and gadflies, so they are often used as a natural biological pest control.

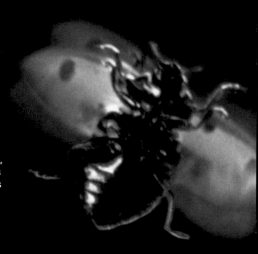

③

Flight

With the elytra open and spread like airplane wings, the second pair of wings is free to move. The muscles at their base control the direction of flight.

②

Takeoff

Although the colorful elytra are not used in flying, the insect needs to lift them in order to unfold its wings, which are seen only during flight.

FRONT VIEW OF ELYTRA

Raised elytra

40-80 inches per second
(1-2 m/s)
AVERAGE SPEED OF FLIGHT

Wings prepared for flight

SEVEN-SPOTTED LADYBUG
Coccinella septempunctata
Thanks to their help in destroying pests, during the Middle Ages these beetles were considered instruments of divine intervention from the Virgin Mary.

The insect is between 0.04 and 0.4 inch (0.1–1 cm) long.

①

Preparation

The elytra can separate from the rest of the body. They protect the thorax, and also the wings when folded inside.

ELYTRON
Name of the modified front wing of beetles

Raised elytron

Visible wing

BACK VIEW

APOSEMATISM
The opposite of mimetism: these insects use their bright colors to scare away danger.

4

Landing

The insect reduces its flight speed. With its wings outstretched, it settles down to touch the surface without gliding. Its hind legs help it to stay balanced.

BODY ARMOR
The elytra are brought close to the body. Then the wings are folded underneath.

IDENTIFYING SPOTS

7 black spots

Adalia bipunctata

Coccinella septempunctata

Chilocorus stigma

Coleomegilla maculata

A QUESTION OF NUMBER
Most insect species, from dragonflies to butterflies, have two pairs of wings. Flies and mosquitoes are among the few exceptions.

FLY
2 wings

BUTTERFLY

4 wings

OTHER FUNCTIONS
Beetles and other insects have two pairs of wings, but with distinct functions.

BEETLES
2 hard elytra

2 wings

CICADAS
(ORDER HOMOPTERA)
2 semi-hard elytra

2 wings

THORAX

HEAD

ABDOMEN

SUPPORT FROM THE LEGS

1 HIND LEGS
remain extended from takeoff.

2 FRONT LEGS
Both pairs can stay flexed until the beetle touches down.

WING

WINGS
Seen only in flight, they fold along a joint in the middle.

ON THE FLOWER
or on the stalks of a plant is where the ladybug finds the aphids it feeds on.

Diving, Swimming, and Skating

or some insects, such as pond skaters in freshwater, or halobates in saltwater, the biblical feat of walking on water is no miracle, but an everyday task. When the waters are calm, the water insect known as a pond skater uses the surface tension of liquid (and certain anatomical features of its body) to do honor to another one of its names: "water strider." But because they need air to breathe, any movement on the surface sends them skittering back to land. Other species have gone further and become divers and swimmers, with mechanisms for breathing and moving underwater. ●

Underwater

There are several aquatic beetle species, with two basic adaptations: the hind legs, in pushing the beetle forward, work like oars, presenting a greater surface area when moving backward than forward, and the elytra can trap air as a reserve for breathing underwater. These species are among the major predators in stagnant freshwater environments. The diving beetle measures about 1.4 inches (3.5 cm) long.

It rises to the surface to fill the air chamber.

Chamber under the elytra

Insect's body

AIR

WATER

DIVING BEETLE
Dytiscus marginalis

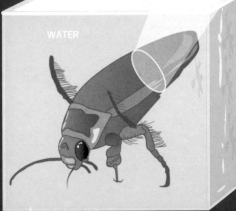

On the Water

Until recently, it was believed that insects of the family Gerridae skated on lagoons and ponds using a type of wax secreted by their legs. Later it was discovered that their feet have large numbers of micro–hairs, 30 times finer than a human hair, that trap tiny air bubbles. The trapped air forms a cushion that keeps their feet from getting wet, and if the feet begin to sink they are buoyed to the surface.

WATER STRIDER
Neogerris hesione
This species lives on freshwater surfaces. It measures 0.5 inch (1.3 cm) long.

MIDDLE LEGS
Used as skates to glide along the water

ANTENNA

FRONT LEGS
are shorter than other pairs. They are used for trapping prey.

SHORT FRONT LEG

SWIMMING LEGS
A system of bristles varies the amount of surface in contact with the water.

Moving forward decreases the surface area.

Moving backward increases the area.

HIND LEGS
provide force to slide
along the surface.

Insects of the order
Heteroptera have divided
wings (hemielytra), with
one half that is hard and the
other membranous.

ABDOMEN

THORAX

5 feet per second
(1.5 m/s)
AVERAGE SWIMMING SPEED

The middle
and hind legs
grow from
separate points
on the body.

CABEZA

THE SURFACE TENSION CAN WITHSTAND

15
times the insect's total weight.

WALKING ON WATER
The legs are arranged on the surface of the liquid in such
a way as to make it an elastic film. The hind legs use this
property for support and traction. Also, the insect supports
itself on segments of its legs, not on just one point.

LEGEND

 X Points of support
on the water

SURFACE TENSION
The mutual pressure
among molecules of liquid
brings the molecules
together so that they
resist pressure that would
penetrate the surface.

Each molecule exerts
pressure in all directions.

AIR

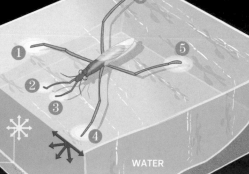

WATER

The angle of contact
between the insect's foot
and the water is 167°.

The middle
pair of legs
is longer.

Metamorphosis

Metamorphosis is the change in shape that insects undergo as they grow. There are two types of transformations: complete, like that of monarch butterflies, and incomplete, like that of dragonflies or grasshoppers. Insects with complete metamorphosis pass through an immobile state (called the pupal, or chrysalid, phase) in which their body is transformed by hormones within a cocoon. ●

1 In the Beginning, the Egg

The adult female lays eggs among the leaves, where they will be protected. Monarch butterfly eggs have colors ranging from grayish-white to cream, and they are shaped like barrels, 0.1 inch (2mm) in diameter. The larvae grow inside the egg until they hatch; after hatching, they eat the shell.

7 days
AMOUNT OF TIME THE LARVA LIVES INSIDE THE EGG

MATING AND EGG LAYING
When monarch butterflies mate, they stay joined all afternoon and evening, until the next morning, for a total of 16 hours. After their first mating, the females lay eggs.

FIVE CHANGES
When it hatches, the insect is shaped like a worm. This caterpillar will molt its exoskeleton five times as it grows in size. Its internal structure will not change, however. Each new exoskeleton is larger than the one before.

Change to pupal phase

Hatching from the egg
The exoskeleton hardens. As the insect grows, the exoskeleton becomes too small. Eventually it splits and falls off.

Fourth shedding

Second shedding

Third shedding

Simple Metamorphosis

Also called incomplete metamorphosis, because, unlike complete metamorphosis, it does not include a pupal phase. The wings and legs develop gradually, so that the insect does not need to spend a certain amount of time immobile. Locusts, cockroaches, termites, and dragonflies have this type of metamorphosis. From an evolutionary standpoint, it corresponds to ancient or primitive insects. One of its characteristics is the nymph stage of young insects. The nymph gradually changes in shape as it grows. When it sheds its exoskeleton, the adult emerges.

EMPEROR DRAGONFLY
Anax imperator

1 EGG

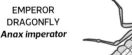
2 NYMPH

3 IMAGO (ADULT)

② Larva or caterpillar

makes its entry into the world by eating its shell. From then on, eating and growing will be its main activities. Every time it sheds its skin, the old exoskeleton is broken. The insect forms a new, soft exoskeleton, which is gradually expanded by blood pressure. The exoskeleton then undergoes a chemical reaction that hardens it.

3 weeks
IS THE AMOUNT OF TIME THE INSECT LIVES IN THE LARVAL STAGE.

A SIMPLE ASSIGNMENT
In the caterpillar phase, the insect focuses solely on eating leaves. In this way it accumulates the necessary energy for the physiological processes of metamorphosis. For digesting the leaves, the caterpillar has a very simple digestive track.

PREPARATION FOR THE PUPAL PHASE
Before passing to the next stage, the larva stops eating and eliminates any food left in its digestive tract. The juvenile hormone, which keeps the transformation of the body in check, starts to become inhibited.

CREMASTER
The caterpillar secretes a fibrous cushion that sticks to the stalk of a plant. It hangs from the cushion with hooks on the end of its abdomen.

HANGING AND IMMOBILE
To leave the larval stage behind and become a pupa, the caterpillar quietly awaits the transformation.

EXOSKELETON
Crossed with yellow, black, and white stripes, it is soft after every shedding and later hardens. The insect always emerges head first.

INSIDE THE LARVA
The insect's heart, nervous system, and breathing system are almost completely developed during the larval stage, and they change very little afterward. The reproductive system is formed later.

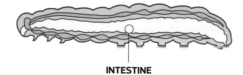

INTESTINE

FAREWELL TO THE OLD BODY
The larva's last exoskeleton begins to fall off and is replaced by a greenish tissue that will form the cocoon, or chrysalis.

Pupa (chrysalis)

After getting rid of its larval exoskeleton, the insect hangs immobile from a branch, protected by a cocoon. Inside, it will develop its distinctive butterfly form. Although it does not eat during this period, it is intensely active biologically and undergoes considerable change. Histolysis, a process in which the larva's structures are transformed into the material that the insect will use to develop adult structures, takes place at this time.

15 days
LENGTH OF THE PUPA, OR CHRYSALIS, PHASE

HISTOGENESIS

New tissues are generated from hemolymph (the equivalent of blood), the Malpighian tubules (the energy-producing organ in insects), and histolyzed tissue, including the larva's muscles. The monarch butterfly pupa is called a chrysalis because of the color and structure of the capsule that protects it. It is oval-shaped with gold and black spots.

BUTTERFLY SHAPE

The adult butterfly's wings and legs develop from the cuticle, or skin tissue, which is composed mostly of chitin. Other organs are preserved or rebuilt from regenerative cells.

HORMONES IN FULL SWING

Metamorphosis is governed by three hormones. One is the cerebral (brain) hormone, which stimulates the prothoracic gland. This gland produces the molting hormone ecdysone, which causes the loss of the old skin. The third hormone is the juvenile hormone, which slows down the transformation to the adult stage.

WITHIN SIGHT

As the time draws near for the adult to emerge, the chrysalis becomes thinner, changes color, and becomes transparent. The transformed insect can be seen inside.

CAMOUFLAGE

The chrysalid capsule has shapes, textures, and colors that help keep it from being noticed, to protect it from predators. The capsules typically resemble leaves or bird droppings.

INTERNAL ORGANS

Inside the chrysalis, the insect's body is changing into that of an adult. The intestine rolls into a spiral shape to assimilate liquid food, and the reproductive organs are developing for the adult stage.

INTESTINE

ANATOMY OF A BUTTERFLY

The body of a butterfly is divided into head, thorax, and abdomen. An adult butterfly's head has four important structures: eyes, antennae, palps, and proboscis. The compound eyes of a butterfly are made up of thousands of ommatidia, each of which perceives light. There are two antennae and the two palps, and they are covered by scales that detect molecules in the air and give the butterfly a sense of smell. The proboscis is a modified tongue through which the butterfly draws nectar and water to feed itself, and it is rolled up when not in use. The thorax is made up of three segments, each of which has a pair of legs attached to it. The second and third segments are also each joined to a pair of wings. Each leg is formed by six segments. When a butterfly lands on a plant, it uses the end segments, called tarsi, to grip the surface of a leaf or flower.

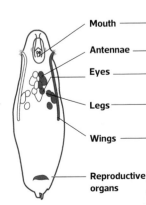

Mouth

Antennae

Eyes

Legs

Wings

Reproductive organs

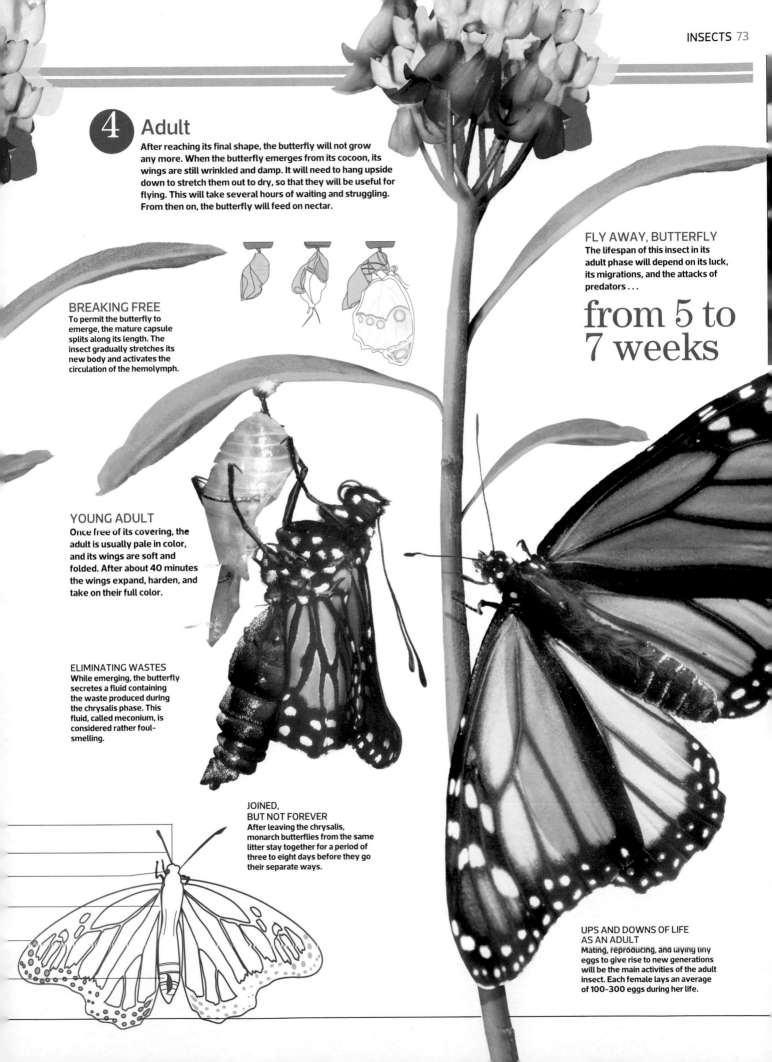

4 Adult

After reaching its final shape, the butterfly will not grow any more. When the butterfly emerges from its cocoon, its wings are still wrinkled and damp. It will need to hang upside down to stretch them out to dry, so that they will be useful for flying. This will take several hours of waiting and struggling. From then on, the butterfly will feed on nectar.

BREAKING FREE
To permit the butterfly to emerge, the mature capsule splits along its length. The insect gradually stretches its new body and activates the circulation of the hemolymph.

YOUNG ADULT
Once free of its covering, the adult is usually pale in color, and its wings are soft and folded. After about 40 minutes the wings expand, harden, and take on their full color.

ELIMINATING WASTES
While emerging, the butterfly secretes a fluid containing the waste produced during the chrysalis phase. This fluid, called meconium, is considered rather foul-smelling.

JOINED, BUT NOT FOREVER
After leaving the chrysalis, monarch butterflies from the same litter stay together for a period of three to eight days before they go their separate ways.

FLY AWAY, BUTTERFLY
The lifespan of this insect in its adult phase will depend on its luck, its migrations, and the attacks of predators . . .

from 5 to 7 weeks

UPS AND DOWNS OF LIFE AS AN ADULT
Mating, reproducing, and laying tiny eggs to give rise to new generations will be the main activities of the adult insect. Each female lays an average of 100–300 eggs during her life.

Order and Progress

A nts are one of the insects with the highest social organization. In the anthill, each inhabitant has a job to do. The head of the family is the queen, the only one that reproduces. All the rest of the ants are her offspring. During mating, queens and drones (males) from various colonies mate on the wing. The queens need to mate several times, because the sperm they receive will have to last their lifetime. ●

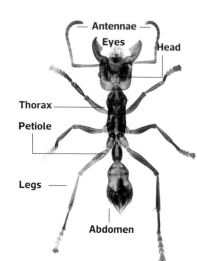

Antennae
Eyes
Head
Thorax
Petiole
Legs
Abdomen

BLACK GARDEN ANT
Lasius niger

MAIN ENTRANCE

The Anthill

After mating, the queen loses her wings and chooses a place to lay eggs. At first she lives on reserves derived from the muscle mass of her wings and some of the first eggs she has laid. She takes charge of raising the first generation of worker ants, which will then take care of finding food while the queen focuses exclusively on laying eggs.

COMMUNICATION

An ant communicates with its antennae through chemical means, by capturing particles of certain substances (pheromones) that enable it to recognize another ant from the same colony. Ants do not have a well-developed sense for perceiving sound.

FOOD STORAGE
Honeypot ants coordinate the food supply.

METAMORPHOSIS

In the egg stage, the future ant remains near the queen but leaves her during the larval stage. Other ants then take care of the larva, and it will become a nymph and form a cocoon to cover itself.

THERE ARE ABOUT

10,000

ANT SPECIES.

EGGS   LARVAE   NYMPHS   COCOON

UNUSED TUNNEL

3 NYMPHS
are fed and taken care of in another area.

2 LARVAE
are carried to another chamber to grow.

1 EGGS
are laid by the queen in the lowest area.

QUEEN ANT

YOUNG ANTS

4 COCOONS
The new ants hatch ready to work.

The Castes

Each ant plays a role in the nest and is assigned its role at birth. Drone, soldier, worker, and replete worker (which stores food reserves) are the castes that distinguish what chores each ant will have.

Four wings

QUEEN
The largest ant. She lays the eggs that will become workers, drones, and new queens.

Two wings

DRONE
His only function is mating; afterward he dies.

WORKER
The worker ant may have the role of gathering food, cleaning, or protecting the anthill.

ANTENNAE
perceive odors and transmit messages.

EYES
can see only a few inches.

VELVETY TREE ANT
Liometopum occidentale

LEGS
Although the legs lack muscles, they are very strong.

JAWS
Weapons for attack and defense

LEGS
Agile and thin

Feeding

Ants cannot eat solid food. The plants and animals they eat are mixed with saliva to form a paste, which is used to feed the whole colony.

Food reserves in abdomen

Storage

REPLETE ANTS

Defense

The most widely used defense is biting and spraying streams of formic acid. Soldier ants have the job of scaring away the enemy because they have larger heads than worker ants.

JAW
The jaw is the ant's main weapon of defense, with a bite that can scare away or harm a rival. The jaw is also used for hunting and feeding.

American farmer ant

Clamping jaw

INTERCHANGE OF FOOD
Having two stomachs, an ant can share food. The transfer begins when the receiving ant uses its front legs to touch the lip of the donor ant.

Stomach Individual pouch

Crop Social pouch

VENOM
may contain formic acid and can kill or paralyze the prey. It comes from special glands in the lower abdomen.

SOUTHERN WOOD ANT
Formica rufa

Poisonous stinger

Abdomen

TRAP-JAW ANT
Odontomachus bauri

Poison sac

Goal: Survival

Evolution has molded some striking traits into living beings. In particular, some insects, disguised as branches or leaves, can escape notice so as to hunt or to hide from predators. To avoid being attacked, other insects develop colors and shapes that deceive other animals and keep them from attacking. Hiding and showing off are two opposite strategies that have been favoring the survival of the fittest for millions of years.●

BRIMSTONE BUTTERFLY
Gonepteryx
The profile of the wings resembles the shape of cut leaves.

PEACOCK BUTTERFLY
Inachis io
The flashy, aposematic (warning) coloration keeps predators away by warning of the danger the insect poses.

WINGS
These wings look like leaves, with a similar color, shape, and structure.

FALSE EYE
The scales are pigmented to look like eyes.

Warning Signals

➤ Mimetism is the imitation of characteristics belonging to dangerous or bad-tasting animals. Replicating the colors and shapes of dangerous animals is known as Batesian mimicry. On the other hand, if an insect produces foul-smelling substances to disgust the predator, that is called Mullerian mimicry.

Defense

The most widely imitated insects are ants, bees, and wasps, because they produce toxic substances that can be deadly.

DOUBLE PROTECTION
Caligo
Owl butterflies combine Batesian and Mullerian mimicry. Predators can confuse the owl butterfly with leaves, but if a predator succeeds in finding it, the butterfly folds its wings to look like the shape and eyes of an owl. The predator, confused, backs off from attacking.

Disguise

These insects use survival strategies designed to keep predators from seeing them. This disguise is their only means of defense.

BODY
Branch-shaped abdomen

AUSTRALIAN STICK INSECT
Extatosoma
This stick-like insect sways back and forth as if tossed by the wind.

LEGS
imitate twigs with dry leaves.

VEINS
In an extraordinary simulation, the veins look like the veins of leaves.

THISTLE MANTIS
Blepharopsis mendica
These mantises use camouflage to hunt unsuspecting insects that get too close to their powerful front legs.

EYES
Compound; enable them to monitor their environment

FRONT LEGS
move slowly so that the prey will not detect them.

Masters of Simulation

Camouflage, or crypsis, is a phenomenon in which animals use amazing disguises as advantageous adaptations. Camouflage is used both by hunters and by potential prey. Insects' bodies may be disguised as various substrates and parts of trees, such as bark, leaves, and branches. These masking techniques are a convenient way for the insect to fade into the background.

One for You, One for Me...

The biological relationships between species can have both positive and negative consequences. One relationship that has good results is mutualism, a relationship between species in which the organisms benefit each other. For example, ants and aphids (plant lice) have established a beneficial interaction. Ants defend and nurture the development of aphid colonies on a plant. In return, the aphids provide a sugary substance to feed their protectors.

KEPT IN RESERVE

Aphids need protection from predators, such as butterfly larvae. Ants pick up eggs and nymphs in their jaws and carry them into their anthills, out of the reach of any predator.

Chain Reaction

The beneficial interaction between aphids and ants can produce secondary effects. In some cases, plants benefit indirectly from the presence of aphid-protecting ants. These guardian insects drive away the herbivores that feed on the tender leaves. In this way, plants invest less energy to replenish their photosynthesizing organs.

Sugar Currents

Generally, aphids form colonies that live on a single plant. They usually place themselves on the underside of a leaf, where the aphids can reach the leaf's veins. The veins carry sugars from the leaves to the remainder of the plant, and the aphids use this flow of sugar as a source of food.

APHID
Extracts nutrients from the leave's ribs with its stylet

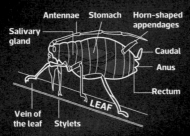

Antennae Stomach Horn-shaped appendages
Salivary gland
Caudal
Anus
Rectum
LEAF
Vein of the leaf Stylets

PARTNERS
Sugars are the product that links these insects.

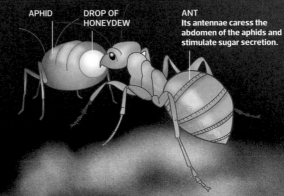

APHID DROP OF HONEYDEW ANT
Its antennae caress the abdomen of the aphids and stimulate sugar secretion.

2,200 pounds (1,000 kg) of honeydew

ARE EXTRACTED FROM A COLONY OF APHIDS BY ANTS EVERY YEAR.

BLACK GARDEN ANT
Lasius niger
is between 0.1 and 0.2 inch (3 to 5 mm) long. The thorax is fused to the first abdominal segment.

BLACK BEAN APHID
Aphis fabae
is between 0.05 and 0.1 inch (1.5 to 3 mm) long. It has very short antennae.

HONEYDEW
is a secretion with a high concentration of simple sugars.

Relationship with People

A piculture, or keeping bees to use their products, is a very old practice. Originally, people only hunted beehives. Not only did they eat the honey from the beehives, they also mixed it with water and left it to ferment so they could make alcoholic drinks. Today the production of honey has been perfected in such a way that

other products, such as pollen, royal jelly, and propolis, or bee glue, are also obtained from the hive. Just as useful as bees, leeches have always been used as therapeutic tools to soothe headaches and stomach upsets. In this chapter you will also learn what happens when insects such as locusts reproduce at dangerous rates.●

The Never-Empty Home

The home can be another place colonized by invertebrates. Some arrive seeking humidity, shelter, or food; others are attracted by the scent of skin, wool garments, or wooden ceilings. Generally, they are considered a threat and are fought, but some can be truly beneficial. There are insects, for instance, that can act as a plague control in the garden. Various strategies can help keep some "ecologic balance" in the home. ●

In the Garden

The home garden is a natural environment in which food chains become established. Species such as snails, which feed on plants, can be destructive. But carnivorous species can keep harmful species at bay. Earthworms and some beetles serve as environmental cleaners because of their eating habits.

LADYBUG
Coccinella septempunctata
eats fleas and gnats.

SNAIL
Helix aspersa
is a nightmare for the green leaves in the garden.

PILL BUG
Armadillidium vulgare

BURYING BEETLE
Nicrophorus

BLACK ANTS
Lasius niger
can go from their nest to the interior of the house.

SPINY-HEADED WORM
Phylum Acanthocephala

EARTHWORM
Lumbricus

Plagues and Illness

When the females feed on human blood, mosquitoes (such as those belonging to the family Anopheles, bearers of malaria) and other insects become vectors for illnesses, since they can transfer microscopic parasites to people. For this reason, bodies of stagnant water, which is where mosquito larvae develop, should be avoided.

BLOODSUCKING BUG (TRIATOMINE)
Triatoma infestans
Triatoma transmits Chagas disease to humans. Chagas disease produces cardiac, digestive, nervous, and respiratory complications. When Triatoma bites a human, it excretes waste on the skin that can contain the parasite Tripanosoma cruzi. The parasite then enters the bloodstream when the victim scratches the bite. This insect lives mainly in makeshift dwellings, between thatched roofs and unbaked bricks.

RUE
Ruta graveolens
Soaked in water this plant repels insects.

THYME
Thymus vulgaris
This herb attracts pollinating bees and repels flies.

HOUSE DUST MITES
Dermatophagoides farinae
Some dust mites carry parasites; others cause allergic reactions.

MOSQUITO
Aedes aegypti
is the vector for yellow fever and dengue fever.

LARVAE

FLIES CARRY AT LEAST
65 infectious illnesses.

"Magic" Carpet

Keeping carpets clean within the home is critical, because few are the insect species that live in a carpet and are nice to humans.

FLEAS
Ctenocephalides

COCKROACHES

CENTIPEDES

A COLONY OF 60,000 TERMITES CAN EAT

2 ounces
(5 g) OF WOOD PER DAY.

AUGER BEETLES
Xylopsocus
The adult beetle lays eggs, and the larva burrows into wood, creating tunnels 0.25 inch (0.6 cm) wide in the wood.

WASPS
Apis mellifera
build their nests (hives) under the eaves.

TERMITES
Nasutitermes
Live inside the wood they feed on.

In the Roof

The wood in roof beams and spaces between them forms a unique environment within a house, especially for the insect order Hymenoptera. Likewise, several species of beetles feed on wood and lay their eggs in it.

TO CONTROL PLAGUES
Many plants, alone or in combination with other plants, are effective and selective.

LAVENDER
Lavandula angustifolia
repels ants (10 ounces in a quart [300 g in about 1 l] of boiled water).

BLOODSUCKING BUG
(TRIATOMINE)

SPIDERS
Their presence indicates that there are many insects in the house.

At Night

Some "inhabitants" of the house avoid daylight and prefer the cover of darkness so they can go unnoticed by people or predators.

ORIENTAL COCKROACH
Blatta orientalis

Afloat with Dust

Dust mites are minuscule arachnids that move among dust particles searching for food. The larvae of the smallest species barely reach .004 inch (100 microns). Ticks are larger and can reach .5 inch (1 cm) in length. Their body is full of grooves that absorb humidity, and their life spans fluctuate between three and four months. They adapt to almost any habitat: marine, freshwater, or land.

0.001 inch (0.2 mm)

DUST MITE
Each of its legs has six parts. It does not fly; the air carries it.

Small, They are Found Everywhere

Dust mites are part of the oldest, most varied, and largest group of animals that have existed since life appeared on the planet—the arthropods—and, within the arthropods, the arachnids. Their body form is highly varied. Contributing to this variety is the arrangement and appearance of their legs and hairs. They can have a thin, elongated body or a short, wide body; their bodies can also be oval, round, cone-shaped, or rhombus-shaped, and the colors depend on the species. There are green, red, violet, orange, and even transparent mites. These insects are distributed throughout the world, and they have adapted to every environment: they live on the ground, in plants, in storage products, in the water, and in the skin of animals.

Liquid Food

When they come in contact with what will be their food, dust mites secrete digestive juices that soften and liquefy solids because their mouth or ingestion system lets them ingest only liquid food.

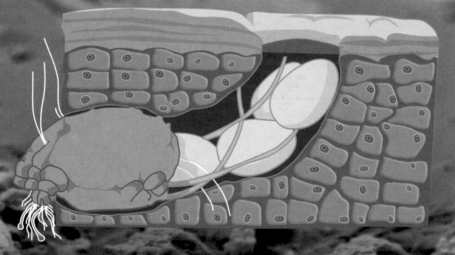

MOUTHPIECES
In these bugs the mouthpieces are in a small front projection, the capitulum (gnathosoma), formed by the appendages that surround the mouth. On each side there is a chelicera that tears, crushes, or bites the food.

1 SARCOPTES MITE
The *Sarcoptes scabei* is a tiny mite that lives under the corneal layer of the epidermis in passages that the female makes in the skin, where she lays her eggs. Between 10 and 14 days later these eggs become adult sarcoptes mites. The presence of this mite under the skin produces intense itching, which can be severe and which can worsen at night. There are special creams and lotions to treat this infection. If boils appear, the infections must be treated with antibiotics.

2 TICK
The tick is the largest acarid; its body has no divisions, and it feeds on the blood of its hosts. It is generally found among tall grasses or in plant leaves, waiting to hook onto any animal or person that passes by. When a tick succeeds in doing so, it uses a hook-like structure in its mouth to penetrate the skin and to begin to suck blood. Once its body swells with blood, the tick lets go.

0.10–0.25 inch (3–6 mm)

Humidity

A fact that many people are not aware of is that the presence of mites is closely linked to humidity. These minuscule animals can cause severe harm at home. They can cause many respiratory illnesses, including asthma. Because dust mites need humid conditions in order to live, every room should be well-ventilated.

HAIRS
come out of the mites' legs. These are actually sensory organs.

3 DUST MONSTERS

House dust mites are so tiny that up to 5,000 of the animals can live in just one grain of dust. Their characteristics include a bulky body, eight short legs, and short sensory hairs. They have appendages next to their mouth that they use to tear or bite and, to their side, pincers with which they hold objects. The body is almost monolithic, practically without differentiation among its parts. Even though dust mites do not bite and are themselves harmless, their eggs and feces cause severe symptoms in people who are allergic to them.

CUTICLE
Even though it is solid and flexible, it must be kept humid.

Flying Waste Matter

The microscopic fragments of fecal matter of the dust mite are carried through the air very easily, blending with dust particles. In this way they are transported for great distances, and they are one of the most common causes of allergic reactions.

Favorite Places

House dust is a conglomeration of small, suspended particles. The content of household dust varies from home to home, and it depends on, among other things, construction materials used and the presence of domestic animals. A dust particle can contain fibrous material, skin scales, animal hair, bacteria, mold, and other natural or synthetic materials. Mites can live among such particles because they feed off those materials.

Beekeeping

The bee is the only insect that humans have kept from antiquity for their own benefit. Thanks to beekeeping, people have been able to collect the honey that bees produce. Honey was the most widely used sweetener in Europe and Asia until the spread of sugarcane during the Middle Ages. With the introduction of new techniques, modern apiculture also obtains pollen, propolis, and royal jelly from bees. Shown here are some details of the basic components of a beehive. ●

Nature's Engineering

Honey is one of the substances that the bees themselves eat. The bees make honey out of flower nectar and pollen from the green parts of plants. They carry the pollen to the hive as a source of protein and use propolin, a tree resin, as a form of antibiotic. Apiculture seeks to promote natural production processes in order to make use of these substances for human benefit.

1 The Bee's Work

Worker bees, the real workers of the hive, carry out their duties from the minute they are born: they build and maintain the cells, feed the larvae and the queen, and clean and protect the hive. Outside the hive, they are in charge of collecting flower pollen and nectar.

SIGNALING
A worker bee finds a source of pollen and lets the rest of the hive know.

THE CHOSEN ONES
Flowers with a good content of glucose and protein.

NECTAR
The bee takes the nectar from the flower, ingests it, mixes it with its saliva, and transports it to the hive.

THE ARTIFICIAL HIVE
has movable panels and frames that permit extraction of the hive's products without destroying the bee colony. This system was invented in 1851 by Langstroth, an American.

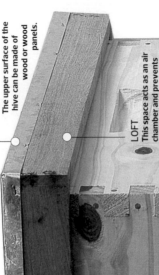

ROOF
The upper surface of the hive can be made of wood or wood panels.

LOFT
This space acts as an air chamber and prevents the sugar super from coming into contact with the exterior.

MOVABLE FRAMES
Each super has about 10 movable frames that are attached to a burr comb with a hexagonal pattern.

60 pounds
(25 kg) of honey
IS STORED INSIDE A HIVE SO THE BEES CAN SURVIVE THE WINTER.

SUPER
is the name given to each detachable module. The upper ones are the sugar supers, and the lower ones are used to raise the young.

HONEY REGURGITATION
The bees deposit honey in all of the cells of the hive.

Open cells with honey

NECTAR, HONEY'S SOURCE

Nectar is made up of 80 percent water and is secreted at the base of the flower's corolla. Honey's flavor depends partly on its aromatic composition, and the beekeeper can select the source of the nectar by changing the location of the hive.

30,000
bees live in a typical hive.

THE POPULATION OF THE HIVE IS KEPT STABLE AS LONG AS NO SUPERS ARE ADDED.

QUEEN SEPARATOR
Worker bees can pass through the separator, but the queen, which is larger, cannot. As a result, honey is stored throughout the hive, but eggs and young bees are found only in the bottom section of the hive.

BROOD CHAMBER
This structure is generally located in the bottom part of the hive.
Their cells include larvae.

FLOOR
Base of the hive

BOTTOM BOARD
This part is placed at a height that will protect the hive from ants or frogs.

Closed cells containing larvae

Queen bee

The queen lays her eggs by moving in a spiral-shaped pattern.

BROOD FRAME
Is the part of the hive used for bee reproduction. Here is where the queen lays her eggs.

OPENING
at the bottom of the hive allows worker bees to enter the beehive chamber where the young are raised. It is located between the floor and the first super.

Worker bee

② Honey Collection
The beekeeper chooses a super, removes it from the hive, and takes out the movable frames by hand. To handle these frames, the beekeeper uses a special suit and other equipment to protect against bee stings. The honey is removed from the detachable frames in a centrifuge, and the frames are then put back into the hive.

THE SUIT
Made of a thick and generally white material. The ventilations are made of double plastic material in both front and back.

Hat and mask with a grille

Some are two-piece suits.

Boots

③ The Smoke
Applied by means of a smoke-producing mechanism, it scares the bees and causes them to eat honey, reducing their tendency to fly and sting.

Smoker

④ Extraction of the Frames
The movable frame system allows for frame removal without affecting the young brood, and the frames can be used again. Before Langstroth's invention, these frames were fixed in place.

The frames are separated from each other by about 0.2 inch (6 mm), the distance between panels in a natural beehive.

From 25 to 50 pounds (11 to 23 kg) of honey are obtained from each super.

The frames have a wire construction.

⑤ The Centrifuge
is a machine that rotates. The honey is heated to a temperature that liquefies it. It is drained from the frames and separated from the wax.

Centrifuge

⑥ Filtering and Bottling
The honey is stored in steel tanks for a week and up to a month to allow any impurities to separate. Bottling and storage require an environment that is dry to prevent the honey from absorbing moisture and that is free of any odors, which might contaminate the honey.

Mechanical centrifuges typically rotate at 200 rpm.

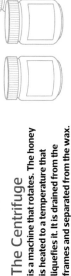

Hungry Together

Under specific environmental conditions, locusts reproduce very rapidly and form a swarm. In Africa, the Middle East, and India locust plagues destroy vegetation and produce great crop losses. Consequently, this type of plague represents a great danger to agriculture and causes great economic loss, hunger, and illnesses in affected populations. Chemical, physical, and biological methods are used to repel the locusts, reducing the harmful effects of the invasion. ●

100 tons

OF VEGETABLES ARE WHAT A MEDIUM SWARM OF LOCUSTS, FORMED BY 50 MILLION INSECTS, EATS IN ONE DAY.

1931

IS THE YEAR WHEN A LOCUST PLAGUE ATE ALL OF THE CROPS AND LEFT CLOSE TO 100,000 PEOPLE DEAD IN NORTH AFRICA.

Locust Plague

The species that causes plagues of locusts on the African continent is the desert locust, *Schistocerca gregaria*. This insect belongs to the Acrididae family and to the order Orthoptera. The locust has an elongated body, about 2 to 3 inches (6–8 cm). The locust modifies its behavior and appearance in response to environmental conditions. It also feeds on most crops, on wild plants, and on some trees, such as sapwoods.

How Does the Plague Start?

When rainfall creates the appropriate conditions for their reproduction, locusts that live in desert or semiarid regions multiply at a dizzying rate. If the species is in the solitary phase, it is harmless, but when rains come and bring about abundant plant life, the locusts gather together, increasing their reproductive capacity. At that point the locusts mutate into their gregarious phase and change not only their movements but also their morphology. Each female is capable of laying 120 eggs, so that an area of 2.5 acres (1 ha) can breed up to 600 million locusts, which will gather into mile-long swarms that travel large distances in search of food.

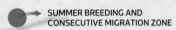 SUMMER BREEDING AND CONSECUTIVE MIGRATION ZONE

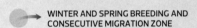 WINTER AND SPRING BREEDING AND CONSECUTIVE MIGRATION ZONE

Locusts reproduce at a rate of millions at a time, and they devour all of the food that lies along their path. The map shows the two main summer breeding zones.

The swarm of locusts moves to other zones in order to reproduce and feed itself. Afterward, during winter and spring, the locusts retrace their path, and the cycle starts over again.

Pest Control

The countries victimized by locusts defend themselves by chemical or biological means on the land or from the air. Pesticide use is restricted, and pesticides can be used against a swarm only when it has begun to form, because misapplication of a pesticide can affect other insects and crops. The locusts are controlled by the application of poisonous bait and by plowing up the ground to bury the eggs.

LOCUSTS IN ANTIQUITY
The devastating effects of locusts can be traced back thousands of years. Locusts were known as one of the seven plagues of Egypt.

Beneficial Vampires

Leeches are worms that have been used as therapeutic tools for thousands of years. History relates that they were used as a remedy for headaches, stomach complaints, eye diseases, mental illness, and other conditions. As the use of drugs increased, the medicinal use of leeches was gradually forgotten. In the 1980s, however, leeches once again began to be used in microsurgery and reconstructive surgery. ●

TEETH

With 300 teeth in its triple jaw, the leech cuts the victim's skin and sucks the blood with its powerful pharynx and the sucker on its mouth. Between the teeth it has glands that secrete hirudin, which keeps the victim's blood from clotting.

MOUTH

THE DECAMERON

Illustration of a chapter of the Decameron by Boccaccio, which shows the use of leeches to treat illnesses. The patient is the Roman emperor Galerius, who has a disease that causes the putrefaction of the body. The three doctors, aghast at his condition, have put leeches on his body to cure him.

SUCKING MOUTH

Once the leech's mouth is placed on the body, it begins to suck blood at the rate of one cubic inch every 2 hours and 40 minutes.

TWISTING

The sections of the leech's body allow it to flex and assume different postures.

Ancient Uses

The use of leeches in medicine goes back over 3,000 years. In Greece, Rome, and Syria these worms were used to remove blood from many areas of the body. It was believed that bloodletting, or phlebotomy, could cure anything from local pains to inflammation and mental disease. In the 18th and 19th centuries, leeches were sold in European pharmacies, and they became very popular in the therapies of the day, especially in France.

FRANÇOIS J.-V. BROUSSAIS (1772–1838)
French doctor who believed that most diseases were caused by the inflammation of the intestines and who preferred bleeding with leeches as a cure. His opinion became so popular that in 1833 he had 40 million medicinal leeches imported into France.

TYPES OF LEECHES

Leeches are classified according to how they feed. One group of leeches includes animals whose pharynx has no teeth and cannot be turned outward. A second group includes leeches whose pharynx is toothless but can be turned outward like an elephant's trunk, projecting out of the leech's mouth, and can be inserted into the host's soft tissues. The third group includes highly specialized leeches in which the pharynx cannot be turned outward but is armed with three chitinous jaws with serrated edges.

1 LEECHES
There are 600 species of leeches. Leeches usually have 34 segments, but they can have 17 or 31. They live mainly in freshwater environments, but a few live in saltwater, and some have adapted to life on land in warm, damp places.

2 EUROPEAN MEDICINAL LEECH
This leech is used in medicine to treat the congestion of veins in reconstructive and plastic surgeries. The bite causes a hemorrhage where the tissue graft is placed, imitating the circulation of the blood.

Lifesaving Saliva

Every time these worms bite a host, substances are mixed into their saliva from glands in their mouth. Anticlotting components, vasodilators, and anesthetics have been identified among these substances, which are extracted and used in clinical medicine. Researchers are also trying to fabricate synthetic leech saliva through the use of bioengineering techniques.

BLOOD CLOT

While feeding on blood, the leech secretes its own anticlotting agents so that the blood will not spoil inside its body while waiting to be digested. Its salivary glands produce hirudin, a specific thrombin inhibitor.

A LEECH CAN ABSORB AN AMOUNT OF BLOOD EQUAL TO

10 times

THE MASS OF ITS BODY.

HOW A LEECH TRAVELS

At either end of the leech is a cavity that the leech can use to attach itself to a surface. To move forward, it attaches one end on the ground and, with an undulating movement, draws the other end toward it.

1
The leech advances its front end and attaches it to the underlying surface. It then draws its rear end forward.

2
When its rear end reaches the attached front end, the leech attaches the rear end to the underlying surface, and the sequence of motions is repeated.

50,000

BREEDING FARM

THE ONLY FARM IN THE WORLD THAT SUPPLIES LEECHES IS LOCATED IN WALES, IN THE UNITED KINGDOM. IT HAS MORE THAN 50,000 LEECHES THAT ARE SHIPPED TO LABORATORIES AND HOSPITALS IN 30 COUNTRIES.

ELASTIC BODY

The segmented body of the leech allows it to move with undulating movements when necessary, for example, to walk. The leech can also put on a show when it is on alert in the presence of a host. At such times it manages to stand itself up on one of its ends.

SUCKER

The leech has two suckers, one at its front end, where the mouth and jaw are located, and another at the rear.

Glossary

Abdomen

Posterior portion of the body of arthropods consisting of similarly formed segments, containing the reproductive organs and a part of the alimentary canal. In insects and arachnids, it is the posterior section of the body.

Adaptation

A structural, physiological, or behavioral trait that allows an organism to live in its environment.

Ambulacral Groove

In echinoderms, any of the radial grooves through which the hydraulic system's tube feet protrude.

Anaerobe

An organism that can live without free oxygen.

Annelids

Animals with a long cylindrical body consisting of ring-formed segments.

Antennae

A pair of long sensory appendages on the head of many arthropods.

Arachnid

An eight-legged arthropod.

Arachnologist

A scientist who studies arachnids-spiders and related groups.

Arthropod

An animal with articulated appendages and a segmented body, covered by an exoskeleton.

Asexual Reproduction

Any reproductive process, such as the production of gemmae or the division of a cell or organism into two or more approximately equal parts, that does not involve gametes joining together.

Bilateral Symmetry

Corporal form whereby the right and left halves of an organism are approximate mirror images of each other.

Biology

The science that studies living organisms-their constitution, structure, function, and relations.

Brachyopods

A group of marine invertebrates whose soft body is protected by a shell consisting of two parts called valves.

Calcite

A form of the chemical compound calcium carbonate.

Carrion Eaters

An animal that feeds on dead animals it finds. Given the occasion, some large carnivores such as lions and hyenas can behave like carrion eaters.

Caste

A social group that carries out specific tasks, characteristic of ants and bees, among other insects.

Celoma

A cavity formed between layers of mesoderm in which the alimentary tract and other internal organs are suspended.

Cephalopod

A class of exclusively marine mollusks with tentacles or legs attached to the head. These appendages have rows of suckers that are used for capturing prey and copulation.

Cephalothorax

The head and thorax combined in one single body segment.

Chelicera

First pair of appendages in crabs, sea spiders and arachnids, usually in the form of pincers or fangs.

Chitin

Tough, durable polysaccharide that contains nitrogen and is found in the exoskeleton of arthropods or other surface structures of many invertebrates, and also in the cell walls of fungi.

Class

One of the many divisions into which scientists classify animals. The invertebrates form a separate class of their own.

Classification

The process of establishing, defining, and ordering taxa within a hierarchical series of groups.

Cocoon

A protective sheath usually made of silk. Many insects make cocoons to protect themselves during the pupa stage, until they become adults.

Colony

A group of animals of the same species that live and work together to survive.

Community

The entire population of organisms that inhabit an environment in common and who interact with one another.

Compound Eye

In arthropods, a complex eye made of many separate units, each of which has light-sensitive cells and a lens that can form an image.

Crustacean

An animal of the arthropod group, with antennae and articulated appendages, that uses gills to breathe and has a body protected by a thick covering.

Cuticle

An organic, noncellular protective covering secreted by the epidermis.

Defecation

The part of an organism's digestive process that consists of eliminating undigested matter.

Dermis

The internal layer of the skin below the epidermis.

Deuterostoma

An animal in which the anus is formed in or near the developing embryo's blastophore zone, and whose mouth is formed afterward in another location; the echinoderms and the chordates are deuterostoma.

Dimorphism

The species that exists in two distinct forms.

Echinoderms

Invertebrate marine animals. The bodies of the adults have a pentagonal symmetry. Underneath the skin they have a calcareous skeleton with spines and protuberances. They have an internal hydraulic system, connected with ambulacral feet, that makes locomotion possible.

Endemic

Native to a particular geographical region and restricted to it.

Endoderm

One of the three layers of the embryonic tissue in animals; it originates in the epithelium that covers certain internal structures.

Epicuticle

The thin, outermost layer of the arthropod exoskeleton, consisting primarily of wax.

Epidermis

The outermost layer of cells.

Epithelial Tissue

Type of tissue that surrounds a body or structure or covers a cavity. Epithelial cells form one or more regular layers with little intercellular material.

Etology

The comparative study of animal behavior in its natural habitat, and the evolutionary, genetic, ecological, and physiological factors that influence its manifestation.

Evolution

The changes in the genetic reservoir from one generation to the next, as a consequence of processes such as mutation or natural selection, among other things.

Exoskeleton

The external covering supporting the body, commonly found in arthropods. It is like an articulated shell made of chitin; it serves as a support for muscles and the soft internal organs.

Eyelet

Simple light receptor, common among invertebrates.

Family

A category in taxonomy that groups genus together; lower than order and higher than genus.

Fossil

The preserved remains of an organism that disappeared a long time ago.

Gamete

The mature reproductive cell that combines with a gamete of the opposite sex to form a zygote that is usually diploid; male gametes are called spermatozoids and female gametes are called ovules.

Gastrovascular Cavity

A digestive cavity with an opening, characteristic of the phyla Cnidaria and Ctenophora. It has digestive and circulatory functions.

Genus

A category in taxonomy that groups species together.

Geotropism

A directional response to gravity.

Gonopore

A pore in the reproductive apparatus through which gametes pass.

Hemocell

A blood-filled cavity inside the tissues; characteristic of animals with an incomplete circulatory system, such as mollusks and arthropods.

Hermaphrodite

An organism that has both reproductive systems, male and female; hermaphrodites may or may not self-fertilize.

Hormone

An organic molecule, secreted in small amounts by one part of an organism, that regulates the function of other tissue or organs.

Host

An organism in which a parasite lives.

Hydrostatic Skeleton

A skeleton in which fluid is contained by muscular walls that transfer the force from one part of the body to another when subjected to pressure.

Invasive

Relating to a species or organism that was brought into an environment and harms biodiversity, agricultural or fishing productivity, or human health.

Invertebrate

Animal without a spinal column. Some, such as worms, have soft bodies. Others, such as arthropods, are protected by a hard exoskeleton.

Kingdom

Taxonomic category that includes phyla or divisions. Until the appearance of the category of domain, the kingdom was the highest-level category in biological classification.

Larva

Animal in a developmental stage, after leaving the egg. It can feed itself but has not yet acquired the shape and structure of the adults of its species.

Mandible

Appendage immediately below the antennae, used to trap, hold, bite, or chew food.

Mantle

In mollusks, the outer layer of the body wall or a soft extension of it. It usually secretes a shell.

Medium

Element or substrate where organisms live.

Mesoderm

The middle layer of the three layers of embryonic tissue.

Metamorphosis

Abrupt transition from the larval form to the adult form.

Metazoa

Main group in the animal kingdom (including mollusks, annelids, and arthropods) in which the mouth is formed at or near the blastula in the developing embryo.

Microorganism

Organism that can be seen only with a microscope.

Migration

Seasonal travel of animals from one region to another to reproduce or to seek food, better climate, or better living conditions in general.

Mimetism

Property of certain animals and plants to resemble living things or inanimate objects that live nearby, mostly by means of color.

Mollusk

Invertebrates of the phylum Mollusca, with a soft body divided into a head, foot, and visceral mass. They have a fold called a mantle that envelops all or part of the body.

Molting

Removal of all or part of the outer covering of an organism; in arthropods, a periodic changing of the exoskeleton that enables them to grow in size.

Nutrients

Chemical elements essential for life. Examples are carbon, oxygen, nitrogen, sulfur, phosphorus, magnesium, and potassium.

Ommatidium

The simple visual unit of a compound eye in arthropods; it contains light-sensitive cells and a lens that can form an image.

Omnivore

Living being that feeds on plants and animals.

Order

Taxonomic category that includes families; category lower than a class and higher than a family.

Organ

Body part made of various tissues grouped into a structural and functional unit.

Organic Material

Animal or plant material in any stage of decomposition, found on or within the soil.

Organism

Any living creature, whether single-celled or multicellular.

Parasite

Organism that lives at the expense of another

Phylum

Taxonomic category that includes classes; category lower than a kingdom and higher than a class.

Plankton

Group of small living beings, whether plants (phytoplankton) or animals (zooplankton), the live suspended in freshwater or ocean water

Planula

Type of unattached, ciliated larva of many organisms of the phylum Cnidaria (jellyfish, sea anemones, and coral).

Polyp

The immobile stage in the life cycle of anim of the phylum Cnidaria.

Population

Group of individuals of the same species th live in a certain area during a specific time.

Predator

Organism that feeds on other living beings.

Pseudocoelom

Body cavity consisting of a fluid-filled space between the endoderm and the mesoderm, characteristic of nematode worms.

Pseudopod

Temporary cytoplasmic projection of an amoeboid cell whose movement and feeding occur through phagocytosis.

Radial Symmetry

The regular disposition of body parts around a central axis in such a way that any plane that cuts through the axis divides the organism in halves that constitute mirror images of each other. It is seen in adult echinoderms.

Safety Thread

Silk thread that a spider leaves behind when is moving, attaching it from time to time to various surfaces.

Salinity

Measurement of the amount of common salt in water or soil. Common salt is a sodium salt, sodium chloride, common in nature, that gives salty flavor to ocean water and salt lakes.

Segmentation

Successive cell divisions in the egg of an animal to form a multicellular blastula.

Sexual Dimorphism

An assembly of external morphological characteristics that make it possible to distinguish the males from the females of the same species.

Sexual Reproduction

Reproduction involving meiosis and fertilization.

Social Insects

Insects that live with others of the same species, looking after the young and gathering food for the community.

Species

A group of individuals that recognize one another as belonging to the same reproductive unit.

Spiracle

One of the external openings of the respiratory system in terrestrial arthropods.

Statocyst

A balance organ consisting of a sac-like structure that contains grains of sand (statoliths) or some other material that stimulates the sensory cells when the organism is in motion.

Substrate

The surface that constitutes an organism's habitat or life support.

Swarm

Insects that act in a group for eating, mating, or finding a new location for a nest.

Tagmosis

The process of segment formation (metameres) into corporal regions (tagmata) with differentiated functions.

Taxism

Also known as taxia, it is the orientation of movement in those organisms that, being able to move freely from one place to another, track their course in the direction of an external stimulus.

Taxonomy

Study of the principles of scientific classification. The organization, grouping, and denomination of living things.

Tentacles

Long and flexible organs located around the mouth of many invertebrates, often prehensile and tactile.

Thorax

In crustaceans and insects, the fused segments located between the head and the abdomen to which the legs are attached.

Tissue

Group of similar cells organized in a structural and functional unit.

Trachea

In insects and some other terrestrial arthropods, the system of air conduits covered with chitin.

Venom

Chemical agent injected into other animals in order to kill or paralyze them, or to ward off an attack.

Zoology

Discipline or science dedicated to the study of animals.

For More Information

American Museum of Natural History
Division of Invertebrate Zoology
Central Park at 79th Street
New York, NY 10024
(212) 769-5100
Website: https://www.amnh.org/our-research/invertebrate-zoology
The Division of Invertebrate Zoology at the American Museum of Natural History studies and archives the living nonvertebrate animals.
    It houses more than 24 million specimens comprising about 500,000 species.

Centers for Disease Control and Prevention
Division of Parasitic Diseases
1600 Clifton Road
Atlanta, GA 30329
(800) 232-4636
Website: https://www.cdc.gov/parasites/
The Centers for Disease Control and Prevention is one of the major operating components of the US Department of Health and Human
    Services. It works to protect America from health threats, both domestically and abroad. The Division of Parasitic Diseases identifies
    common and uncommon parasites and diseases they cause and provides information on how to seek medical attention.

Entomological Society of America
3 Park Place, Suite 307
Annapolis, MD 21401
(301) 731-4535
Website: https://www.entsoc.org
The Entomological Society of America is the largest organization in the world serving the professional and scientific needs of entomolo-
    gists and individuals in related disciplines. It publishes eight journals that provide coverage of the broad science of entomology.

Entomological Society of Canada
503-386 Broadway
Winnipeg, MB R3C 3R6
Canada
(888) 821-8387
Website: http://esc-sec.ca
The Entomological Society of Canada promotes, advocates, facilitates, and communicates research and education on insects and their
    relatives, mentors the development of younger entomologists, and showcases Canada's entomological expertise nationally and interna-
    tionally.

The Xerces Society for Invertebrate Conservation
628 NE Broadway, Ste. 200
Portland, OR 97232
(503) 232-6639
Website: https://xerces.org
The Xerces Society is an international nonprofit organization that protects wildlife through the conservation of invertebrates and their
    habitats. They work with partners including scientists, land managers, educators, policymakers, farmers, and citizens to facilitate habi-
    tat conservation and restoration, species conservation, protecting pollinators, contributing to watershed health, and reducing harm
    from pesticide use.

For Further Reading

Baum, Margot, and Jennifer Viegas. *Parasites* (Germs: Disease-Causing Organisms). New York, NY: Rosen Publishing Company, 2017.

Bradley, Richard A. *Common Spiders of North America.* Berkeley, CA: University of California Press, 2012.

Brusca, Richard C., Wendy Moore, and Stephen M. Schuster. *Invertebrates* (Third Edition). Oxford, UK: Oxford University Press, 2016.

Cowles, Jillian. *Amazing Arachnids.* Princeton, NJ: Princeton University Press, 2018.

Despommier, Dickson D. *People, Parasites, and Plowshares: Learning from Our Body's Most Terrifying Invaders.* New York, NY: Columbia University Press, 2016.

Li, Judith L., and Michael T. Barbour, eds. *Wading for Bugs: Exploring Streams with the Experts.* Corvallis, OR: Oregon State University Press, 2011.

Lockwood, Jeffrey. *The Infested Mind: Why Humans Fear, Loathe, and Love Insects.* Oxford, UK: Oxford University Press, 2013.

Middleton, Susan. *Spineless: Portraits of Marine Invertebrates, the Backbone of Life.* New York, NY: Abrams, 2014.

Rodríguez, Ana María. *Vampire Bats, Giant Insects, and Other Mysterious Animals in the Darkest Caves* (Extreme Animals in Extreme Environments). New York, NY: Enslow Publishers, Inc., 2012.

Simon, Seymour. *Insects.* New York, NY: HarperCollins, 2017.

Index